lecturing

a practical guide

sally brown & phil race

KOGAN
PAGE

First published in 2002

Kogan Page Limited
120 Pentonville Road
London N1 9JN
UK

Stylus Publishing Inc.
22883 Quicksilver Drive
Sterling VA 20166–2012
USA

British Library Cataloguing in Publication Data

A CIP record for this book is available from the British Library.

ISBN 0 7494 3671 9

Typeset by Saxon Graphics Ltd, Derby
Printed and bound in Great Britain by Biddles Ltd, Guildford and King's Lynn
www.biddles.co.uk

Contents

Foreword

If you give lectures you may find yourself pictured within. What's worse, others may recognize you when you don't!

Every university has a few Professor Oakwoods. This professor is well intentioned and conscientiously worked hard at lectures when first putting them together, but has become complacent and unwilling to learn any of the new tricks now available. Underneath there's some yearning after yesteryear and a primary interest in research and students who will go on to be research collaborators.

Dr Arbuthnott on the other hand enjoys giving a performance with all the latest technology. The only trouble is that admiration of the performance has become more important for this lecturer than students' learning from it.

In contrast Bill hates lecturing and is so nervous that he went from bad to worse and stayed there in spite of all his attempts to prepare his subject matter thoroughly. He really needs some help from colleagues or the staff development unit, but is too embarrassed to ask and fears even more embarrassment if he did. He responds well to students in small groups or the lab and would do better using that strength in lecture classes rather than trying to give a performance.

Louise is always in a rush, not fully prepared, dashes in, and gives the appearance of being disorganized.

Anya Wilenska brings with her the values and expectations of her native country where lecturers deliver lectures of a high academic standard, without interruptions, to large classes and leave students with the responsibility of studying to understand them. To adjust to their needs is, for her, to compromise those standards.

Though not as portraits, there is an equally characteristic set of students' comments. But I must say no more, or I will spoil your enjoyment of the book.

One of the great virtues of this book is the accessibility of the practical advice it contains. It is an orchard among others in its field. Each chapter is a tree that can be viewed as a structure on its own. On nearly every tree there are bullet points of fruit. You may harvest them all at once and store them in your memory for use when you need them; or when hungry for a particular piece of advice you may survey them all on the tree and pluck one or more that most satisfies your immediate need.

The way I would use this book is to view the plan of the orchard as a whole and then go to a particular tree, survey the fruit and note what is available without committing them all to the store. Then when I have need, I will know where to go for what I want.

But not everyone works in the same way. Some will begin at the beginning and work through systematically. Others may do that for specific chapters and neglect the rest. You could, like students deriving pleasure from observing a demonstration without making the effort to learn anything from it, simply enjoy the portraits I mentioned without doing any of the hard work. That's a temptation like looking at the pictures without getting to grips with their significance. We've all done that sometimes.

Yet the hard work is worth it. Sally Brown and Phil Race offer the fruits of considerable experience in helping lecturers young and old. They have written widely on lecturing, *The Lecturers' Toolkit* and *2000 Tips for Lecturers* (both published by Kogan Page) being particularly well known. They have a combined half-century of working in higher education and have run workshops on lecturing with over a thousand academic staff. In preparing this book they consulted more than 200 people who have contributed their ideas and experience.

Furthermore you will find advice, indeed whole chapters, on topics hardly covered elsewhere in the literature. The chapter on disabilities is a case in point. The section on architecture is another. The chapter on linking up with other areas of the curriculum covers another area that needs more exploration than it has received hitherto. Finally, the authors write in the context of new methods of electronic communication that even they could not have anticipated 10 years ago.

I commend this book to every lecturer.

Donald Bligh
dabligh@ex.ac.uk

Acknowledgements

Our special thanks go to Deb Chapman for her research and administration: the book owes a lot to her meticulousness, patience and hard work.

We are also very grateful to Lawrie Phipps and Alan Hurst who gave us expert comments on drafts of our chapter on inclusive lecturing, and added many valuable points.

Thank you too to Donald Bligh for his Foreword and comments on the manuscript. Donald is author of the classic on lecturing *What's the Use of Lectures?*, the latest edition of which was published in 2002 by Intellect Books, Bristol.

Thanks to the following participants and others at the Belfast ILT Members' Forum (December 2001) who contributed ideas and helped us to pilot the draft case study personae: Vicky Davies, M Murphy, D Brennan, N Yeates, Lorraine Stefani, Alan Robinson, Dorothy Black, John Millikan, James Umomoibhi and Chris Strugnell. Thanks also to participants at the South East Region ILT Members' Forum at Canterbury (also in December 2001) who similarly piloted draft case studies.

Thanks too to the contributors who supplied definitions of 'lecturing' for Chapter 2 and who gave their names, including, in alphabetical order: Alison Holmes; Andrea Rayner; Angela Wilde; Angus Race; Ben Knights; Ben Marsh; Bernard Lisewski; Bob Johnson; Bob Mathew; Caroline Walker-Gleaves; Charles Juwah; Chris Kershaw, Chris Osborne; Clara Davies; Dave Jessop; Dave Wadsworth; David Anderson; David Douglas; David Grantham; Debbie Carter; Dennis James; Diane Bradley; Eileen Barrett; Fran Carfield; Gaelle Villejoulent; George Magoulas; Georgina Sear; Gerry Turvey; Gill Presland; Harsha Buddhden; Hazel Chalmers; Hazel Jamieson; Helen Douglas; Ian Rogerson; Ilze Grickhus; Jane Mace; Janet Wellard; Jesus

Angel Miguel Garcia; Jim Blythe; Jim Rawe; Jo Lay; Joe Holden; John Cowan; John Jones; John Shackleton; John Simms; Jyoti Choudri; Ken Hudson; Lawrence Hamburg; Lesley Gibson; Lesley MacDonald; Lewis Elton; Linda Wilson; Lindsay Brigham; Lionel Adey; Lynn Gabrielson; Maggy McNorton; Mark Nichols; Mark Rogerson; Mary Richards; Maurice Gledhill; Michael McCabe; Mick Healey; Mike Holmes; Mike Routledge; Mike Ryan; Muriel Adey, Oliver Phillips; Patrick Smith; Paul Sherman; Pete Brown; Peter Schwartz; Philip Stanier; Richard Blackburn; Richard Smith; Robert Ariens; Robert Edwards; Rod Webster; Roni Bamber; Ruth Soetendorp; Sandra Rennie; Stuart McAnulla; Tina Overton; Victoria Yorke; Viv Lever; Wendy Stainton-Rogers; Zazie.

We also thank Peter Davies, whose useful leaflet provided some background information.

Thanks also to the anonymous contributors.

Sally Brown and Phil Race

1 Introductions

This book is designed to help lecturers, both new and experienced, to unpack the aims and activities associated with lecturing. We were drawn to the topic because lecturing still remains the most common form of curriculum delivery in higher and further education, despite the number of critics who question its value, and despite the whole range of technological means of delivering content to students electronically that are available to us nowadays.

We have populated this book with a group of fictional lecturers (and their students) to illustrate key points in each chapter. Although the words we put into their mouths are not verbatim quotes of real people, the language they use and the ideas they express are easily recognizable, both to us and to colleagues in workshops on lecturing with whom we have trialled elements of this book (our thanks to them; see the earlier acknowledgements). In our combined 60-odd years of giving lectures in higher and further education, and of meeting and working with many thousands of lecturers and their students, we have recorded and noted the kinds of comments which you read here in the personae we use to bring the issues to life. The soundbites were developed by aggregating remarks and comments that we have heard, overheard, had reported to us or read in student feedback, and on some occasions said ourselves. Once we have introduced these characters to you, we will go on in Chapter 2 to review a series of definitions we have received from over a hundred real respondents to our question, 'What is lecturing?' After this, we will look at some of the background and context to lecturing, before rehearsing the most important reasons why we have lectures, drawing here on some of the extensive literature in the field.

Next, we systematically work through what lecturers can do in lectures, what tools we can use to get our message across, what activities students can be involved in doing to make sure that learning (not just teaching) happens, and what both students and lecturers can do prior to and after lectures. We then go on to explore the links between lecturing and other learning activities, as well as issues around how to support students with special needs in our lectures. We draw to a conclusion with a range of ways we can evaluate and review our lecturing, before a postscript in which our dramatis personae make a final appearance.

First then let us introduce you to our hopefully representative lecturers' voices, and to what some of their students might say about them. The characters we are introducing here are all hard-working dedicated academics, as are the vast majority of real lecturers we have worked with over the years. Struggling against the increasingly heavy and competing pressures of research, teaching and administration (and often management), it is a difficult and demanding job.

the lecturers ...

Dr D

I don't understand it. The students have given me pretty bad feedback again this year, you see. I don't think it's my accent – they don't complain about that. The students are very friendly to me in the lab, and they invite me to their Society socials. I just want them to learn the subject well, but they say they don't understand it. I know my material – I'm regarded highly at the conferences, and there everyone understands me. I give the students my papers too, and I can't see how they can't get the hang of what I am telling them. None of them is stupid, they all come in with good A level scores and this material isn't particularly difficult. I'm completely baffled. And attendance is getting bad. Some mornings I seem to be speaking to a half-empty room.

students' views ...

He's a brilliant man, but he shouldn't really be teaching students like us. He is much too clever. He should be working with postgraduates really, since he is going way over our heads.

I make a good set of notes in his lectures, but when I read them back, they mean nothing to me, because I just don't understand the concepts. He doesn't go too fast or anything, he just doesn't seem to be able to come down to our level. It makes me feel really stupid.

Actually, I've stopped going to his lectures as I get more from reading the textbook. I find going to his classes just confuses me.

the lecturers ...

Professor Oakwood

I've always had good feedback from students in the past – I've been at it for long enough to know what I'm doing, surely. They pass their exams. Some of them come through to research with me. I enjoy lecturing and take it seriously, much more so than many of my colleagues. But students today are from the MTV generation, they expect to be entertained rather than taught and they seem to have very short attention spans. They also don't seem to want to put the work in and expect me to hand everything to them on a plate. If I give them all my overheads as they request, they sit there in class doing nothing, so I think it better that they make their own notes. I could go on a course, I suppose, and find out how to put all the notes on the Web, like some of my colleagues, but I can't see how that will help. I try to get them really interested in the subject, but not all of them are bright enough to cope with the material nowadays.

students' views ...

Professor Oakwood is from the old school and makes no concessions to students. You are expected to sit there in class and write it all down, including really complicated diagrams which you are supposed to copy in record time while at the same time listening to the theory behind it all. It is as if photocopying hadn't been invented. We've asked for back-up handouts so we don't get writer's cramp, but we always get fobbed off.

I've found some really good stuff on the Web site of the department where my girlfriend is studying, so I've started to rely on that a lot for background material. It's not an identical match to what we have on our course, but it's better than being back in the dark ages in our place where the most complex technology available seems to be the biro!

I wonder if Prof Oakwood has ever been held captive as a hostage or something. It's mesmerizing watching the pacing, three steps to the right, turn, look at the screen, three steps to the left, glance at notes, three steps to the right... It's tempting to run a sweepstake on how many cross-rostrum passages are completed in the hour. And it's very distracting too.

What I really hate are Professor Oakwood's attempts at jokes. They're not racist or sexist or anything, they just rely on appalling puns or references to 'chart toppers' from the 60s and 70s. My mum might enjoy them, but I don't! And the anecdotes from the old days! You just want to shout, 'Cut the crap, Prof, and get on with the lecture' but fortunately we're all too polite.

Bill

It's all those eyes! All watching me. I know what I'm talking about – that's not the problem. I've prepared it well enough – I've typed it all out, and edited it, and read it out to get the timing right, and printed it out large so I can read it without bending down over the lectern. It takes me ages to prepare each lecture. It's their eyes. My throat just dries up and my voice goes down to a squeak. I start to sweat like a pig. My eyes water and I can't see my script properly. It's fine in the lab, I really enjoy talking to ones and twos and helping them get going. They're bright students and trying really hard. I watch other people giving lectures, but it doesn't help me. Sometimes they seem to be saying nothing at all, but don't get flustered. I'm trying to say a great deal, but it gives me nightmares. I feel I'm just not cut out to be up there on the rostrum in Theatre 2. It's not my place.

It's painful to watch him really. He is obviously really suffering in front of us. We can't hear what he says because he's so nervous, his voice drops at the end of the sentence and what he is saying just vanishes into the ether, even though he is using the microphone. And those flickering eyes. He keeps looking up, catching sight of the audience and then obviously panicking. He shouldn't wear dark-coloured shirts either, because you can watch the patches of sweat spreading as he gets more and more het up. I don't think he's cut out for the job, really.

I like him and he really knows his stuff, but it's difficult to listen to him because he makes a lot of stumbles, especially with the long words. He doesn't do that in the problem sessions, so it's obviously 'performance anxiety'! He'll probably be ok by the time we get into the final year, but can we wait until then?

He just reads the stuff out, but there's no point in being there really as he puts his notes on the Web, so I just stay in bed for his 9 o'clocks and print it off later so I can read it at a more sensible time of day. From what people tell me, I'm not missing much.

the lecturers ...

Salima Theodocus

Last person in to the department gets the worst timetable, I suppose. I guess everyone has the garbage to do when they first start. I'd never even done phase equilibria when I was a student. Surely it's not as important as thermodynamics. And it's just service teaching – what do these engineers need with it? Fortunately, Pete gave me his notes. He did it for the last three years, since he first started, but has now moved upwards and onwards to thermodynamics. Now it's my turn. I've redone his notes a bit, but they seem fine to me. I guess I'll get by using these. Honestly, I just haven't time to go and read a book on it just now – the first lecture's tomorrow – and I only found that out yesterday!

students' views ...

We've just started getting her and she's useless, can't answer any of our questions and just keeps saying, 'I'll come back to that in a later lecture' but she never does.

She just seems to be going through the motions. I can put up with a lot from someone who obviously cares about what they are doing, but she seems as bored as we do. How are we supposed to be interested when she obviously isn't? And I reckon she is getting things wrong, because I looked up some of the things she said in the textbook we were recommended and her version seems all jumbled up to me. Saying that, there were some of her slides that were word for word from the textbook. And they go on at us about plagiarism!

the lecturers ...

Louise

I've been here 18 months now and it doesn't seem to be getting any easier. I'm still overwhelmed with work and still only keeping a couple of weeks ahead of the students with the lecture preparation. It was so much easier when I was a postgrad doing a few seminars. I thought I had really cracked it then, so when I got the lecturer's job, I thought it would be a doddle. But the relentless pressure of preparing lectures is driving me into the ground. I always seem to be up half the night before my big Thursday lecture with the final years, so that by the time I get into the lecture room, I'm shattered. And the technician gets so cheesed off with me if I don't book the right equipment well in advance, but honestly, I don't always know when I'll need a video or whatever until I've done my preparation. And even if I am well ahead of myself, I still don't seem to manage to get my photocopying requests in to the office in time. I suppose I ought to get it all done before term starts, but that is when I have to get my field trials done, and there just doesn't seem to be enough time. Anyway, it's always such a relief when the lectures finish, I tend to forget about it all until the beginning of term looms up again like an iceberg coming out of the mist!

students' views ...

She rushes in at the last minute with an armful of books and articles, showering papers in her path and dropping overhead transparencies on the floor so they are all out of order before she starts. No wonder she gets flustered. So we all wait patiently while she organizes herself and then she's off like a rocket. The only rest we get is when she loses her place and we get a couple of minutes while she randomly shuffles everything before we're off again!

If I ran my life like she runs hers, I'd not get anything done. Before I come in to class, I've got everyone up, the kids off to school, two loads of washing on the line and the supper for that evening sorted out. She comes in late, looking as if she's just got out of bed and fiddles on for 10 minutes trying to work out what she is doing. It makes me sick that I've killed myself to be in by 9 o'clock and she hasn't got the courtesy to at least be ready to start on time. And then she over-runs, eats in to the 10 minutes we need to get across the campus to our next class, and wonders why we all rush out like rats out of a trap as soon as she asks if we have any questions.

I get annoyed that there doesn't seem to be any system to the order in which we do the lectures. It would be ok if she did the topics in chronological order, or by themes or whatever, it wouldn't really matter. And true enough, when you sit down and look at the course handbook, she covers all the stuff sooner or later, but I would be able to make more sense of the content if I could see where it was all leading. You have to wonder whether she has any idea herself sometimes. It's a shame really, because what she talks about is really interesting and she's good at getting her enthusiasm across when she puts her mind to it.

The handouts are good when you get them, it's just you sometimes don't see them until a couple of weeks after the lecture concerned. She tends to bring a big pile of them in together and hand them out in bundles, and you are not always sure you've got everything so you tend to grab everything you see and sometimes end up with several copies of the same thing. Then, with the best will in the world, you stuff them into your file with every-thing else, and then when it gets near the exam, you bring them all out and try and put them into some kind of logical order but by that stage, it all seems so long ago, it just gets confusing.

the lecturers ...

Arthur

In the old days we'd never have done this stuff in a lecture theatre. We had at most 20 students, and they were really keen. They came because they wanted to learn. We had time to talk to them then. But now with so many of them, what can we do? I've been told I've got to give them lectures and I've done my best really, but I'm still not convinced it's a good way to get them thinking about how to improve their own art. Only some of them really want to go on with the topic. And how can I show them things in a tiered lecture room like that? It's ok for the ones in the front two rows, they can see what I'm showing them. They seem to be the keen ones anyway. It's when I look up to those further back – their faces are blank, they've glazed over. And the ones who aren't interested seem to always sit at the back – and they chatter. I get really annoyed when they chatter. Anyway, I don't think my subject lends itself to the lecture format. What am I supposed to do, tell them which way up to hold a paintbrush?

students' views ...

I don't believe this guy! He comes in with a pile of postcards and a couple of textbooks and gets us to pass them around while he's saying something about the artist, but by the time they get to us at the back, he's about seven paintings further on, so it's hard to link up what he is saying with what we're looking at. It would be ok if we could freeze-frame him while we wait for the stuff to get to us! And he really goes off it if we try and check with each other which one it is he is referring to, so it's easier just to sit back and let it all wash over us.

We call it 'talking in other people's sleep'! He comes in with a carousel full of slides, most of them nothing to do with the subject he's supposed to be talking about, and rambles on in the hot room with the lights off. Honestly, yesterday I could hear three people snoring. He ought to realize that some of us are knackered before we start. I do the early shift stacking shelves at the supermarket before I come in to college, so I need something to wake me up a bit.

You'd think that having been in the business as long as he obviously has, he would have managed to master the slide projector. We took bets one week as to how many would be upside down, back to front or whatever, and I won with my guess of 26. He even had a slide catch fire in the projector once. And he keeps saying, 'Is it in focus?' and when we tell him it isn't, he faffs on for 10 minutes and still doesn't get it right. And in the dark, we can't write down anything he says, so we forget who did all the pictures and stuff.

I just don't see the point of sitting in lectures, and I don't reckon the lecturer does either. I didn't come here to do lots of writing, I came here to do my own work. I've always liked making art rather than trying to put things into words. If I'd wanted to write essays and stuff I'd have done English or something. So trying to make notes in lectures is a night-mare. When I try to read the stuff back later, it's just garbage. I've tried going to the library to look up some of the artists he's talking about and I have to flick through looking for pictures I recognize, since the names I've written down are nothing like how they appear in the book. I spent ages looking for the Norwegian guy, Munch.

I sit with someone from my own country whose English is not very good but when I was trying to translate for her last week, the lecturer shouted at me to shut up. I don't think this a polite way to treat students, and I am going to make a complaint.

the lecturers ...

Anya Wilenska

Students in this country show no respect for the teacher. My English is just fine – I'm told it's better and clearer than most of my English colleagues! I've got a good voice. They can hear every word in the back corner of Theatre 3. I ask them questions – and they answer. But they drive me insane with their stupid questions, they interrupt me all the time and haven't got the courtesy to wait until I have finished my presentation. I do my work before the lecture. I've got all the slides on PowerPoint, and I check from the back that every word is visible. I don't print out handouts with the slides on – I tried that, but there were complaints about the photocopying budget. So I put them on the intranet, and students can download them and print them off, or keep them on their own computers.

Is it the students? In my country, you wouldn't look up and see them nodding off! You wouldn't see the ones at the back texting with their mobiles. Can't they see that the slides are just the questions? It's what I say that they need to be thinking about – but they don't think. Why don't they make notes, these students? I've told them that the slides are just the skeleton.

students' views ...

All I want is a decent set of notes from her lectures. It's not a lot to ask! She comes across as all hoity toity and when you ask a simple question of clarification, she treats you like an idiot. She obviously hates students and can't wait to get away at the end of the class, so there's no chance to speak to her and ask her things. And she's so sensitive: if you don't understand the way she says something, she gets on her high horse about how she speaks seven languages when that wasn't what you meant at all!

She goes at such a pace that it's impossible to think and write at the same time. There is so much information in there, but she doesn't relate it to anything we've done already so you're sitting there, trying to make sense of all this random data she's throwing at you and you feel really stupid because although the words in themselves make sense, I just can't fathom what she is getting at.

If you look at her notes on the Web, which I've tried to do, it's just a big list of names and concepts and dates and movements, but nothing connecting them together. It's just her bullet points from the lecture, and if I'd understood it then, there would have been no need to come back to it later!

the lecturers ...

Marisa

I can't stand all this educational jargon hoo-haa! I'm fed up of trying to jump through all these quality hoops and write in QAAhili! The thing I really like is when like today there's something in the newspaper which I can use in my lecture. It brings it all to life. There's nothing better than a good story. It's great in Theatre 2 – there's the doo-dah which you can use for your overheads, but you can put the paper directly onto it, and bingo, project it up there for all to see on the big screen. It took me a bit of practice to master the thing, but now I can focus in quickly and show the article – and the photos if there are any – big enough for everyone to read even at the far back – I've checked. I used to photocopy things for the students, but had the frighteners put on me by the session we had on copyright, so now I am super careful.

But you just can't satisfy some of them. 'How does all this fit in with what we are going to get in the exam?' one of them asked me last week. 'What about the learning outcomes?' Stuff the learning outcomes, this article is the real thing. This is what my students need to be thinking about today – it's happening now. 'Didn't state the learning outcomes at the start of the lecture' – of course I didn't, this wasn't around when we wrote the course. 'Didn't link the lecture material to the assessment tasks.' For goodness sake, I've written their exam for 20 years, and I think I know how to do it by now!

And they say that the feedback written on their essay scripts doesn't link to what I've been telling them about in the lectures. But I don't give them feedback these days – that's done by the postgrads who don't even sit in my lectures, they haven't got time. In any case, they know best how to talk to students – they remember being students not long ago – they've got time to spend giving students feedback – I can't possibly talk to all 224 of the students in this group. Of course I can't link what I say in class to the exam – I wrote that two months ago, but what's more important, making the material immediate and topical, or tying it all up to documentation we wrote months or even years ago? Surely that's what lectures are for, bringing it all to life?

And it's not easy to see how exactly I'm supposed to make my lectures fit in with Jim's. I know that in the exam we write half each, and students have to do two questions from each section. But this year only one student did three of mine and two of Jim's – all the rest did three of his. I get on fine with Jim – he's a good lecturer and cares for our students – but so do I. But they say that they don't know what they're supposed to be doing for me. Perhaps Jim does spoon-feed them. They don't need spoon-feeding – they're perfectly able to make sense of it. I can't tell them everything. They need to be able to find things out for themselves – surely that's what it's all about.

students' views ...

I'm making real financial sacrifices to be here at university and I can't afford to mess around. I'm all in favour of reading round and getting the big picture but it's really difficult for me to get to the library more than once in a blue moon so I need the lectures to give me the basics. If I'm taking on all this debt, I need to know I'm getting a good degree out of this, so I keep a very careful eye on the course booklet so I know what I have to do. It's not that I'm not interested in a current affairs take on the subject, but that's the kind of thing I can do in my own time. In class I need to be really focused.

This lecturer tries to be very topical, but I get fed up with the fact that all the examples she chooses are from England. Anyone would think the rest of the world didn't exist. There are many international students in this class, but all we ever hear about is what's happening in the business world here. It's often not even the most interesting material around, but she's so Eurocentric, she can't see beyond her own tiny world.

I think she's lazy really. She doesn't do proper preparation, just picks up whatever comes to hand and rambles on about it. You can't be sure what you are supposed to write down and last year the students in the year before us put in a formal complaint that their degree results were affected because there were great big gaps in what she was supposed to have taught them. It was all hushed up of course and she got away with it by saying students were supposed to 'read for' the degree and 'take responsibility for their own learning' or some such rubbish. But as far as I'm concerned, it just stinks and I shan't do any of her courses in the future.

the lecturers ...

Dr Arbuthnott

I really look forward to my lectures – they're very much at the heart of what I do with my students. Having them all together is such an opportunity to really enthuse them and fire them up to follow things through. I've long since felt comfortable in lecture theatres, especially when I'm in one with all mod cons. If it's there, I tend to use it – that goes for video, live Web links, and of course things like PowerPoint – I'd be lost without that now. I used to have files and files full of snazzy transparencies, but I've archived them now, as they go out of date so quickly. With PowerPoint, I can update my slides before and after every lecture I give, and often make adjustments to them during the lecture. I'm known for adding new things there and then in front of all the students – it's a good job I learnt to touch type as a postgraduate.

I try to capture their imagination and make them think. I've read all about the importance of visual learning, and try to make the most of it. When I'm giving a large group lecture, I really enjoy myself – and the students seem to enjoy it too – you can tell. I often dream I'm giving lectures, but sometimes have nightmares about the server going down or the projector bulb blowing – but it hardly ever actually happens these days.

I'm only too happy to have colleagues sit in on my lectures – I guess I like to interest them in just what they too can do with the technology in the theatres. It would be a shame just to stand there and lecture, with all the things we can now do to make it interesting for students.

---

students' views ...

No one could argue that Dr Arbuthnott fails to present the material effectively. Trouble is, it's a bit like going to the movies: it feels like a total experience while you're watching it happen, but then it's all gone the minute we walk out the door.

I'm never very sure what we're supposed to be doing in the lecture, and I don't even bother taking notes any more, there's no point, all the slides are on the Web even before the session. Mind, I don't always get round to downloading and printing them myself, as there's pages and pages of them, which is expensive, because we are only given a card for 500 copies on the printer each semester for the whole course, after that we pay for additional stuff ourselves.

Lots of the other lecturers could take lessons from Dr Arbuthnott on presentation skills. It's fired me up to learn how to use a presentation manager in similar ways in my own seminar presentations, even though it's always a pain trying to get a data projector set up in the room just for my bit – everyone else uses the overhead projector. Nevertheless, I admire professionalism and you don't get much better than this!

I once tried to ask Dr A a question, but it was obviously out of order because it disrupted the schedule of the performance. I don't find that very helpful, because unless I can ask questions when I'm struggling, I don't really feel as if I'm learning. It's all very well being told to go away and look it up on the relevant bits of the Web site after the session, but it's in the lecture itself that I'm struggling to make sense of the concepts. It feels like a waste to lose that momentum, even though I know it isn't possible to answer everyone's questions all the time. All the same, I guess if I'm battling, others will be too.

These are our dramatis personae, not real people but realistic, we are told by those who have helped us to develop them via workshops. In the rest of this book we will use these voices to characterize problems, challenges and difficulties that are faced by lecturers everywhere, and we will try to suggest some approaches and techniques that might be helpful.

2 What is 'lecturing'?

One way of finding out what 'lecturing' means is to consult a dictionary – or several dictionaries. We'll leave this to you to do! We tried it, but it wasn't very helpful to us in the context of trying to write a book about lecturing, or particularly on how to do lecturing well.

Our instinct led us to ask a range of people – over a hundred – what they thought 'lecturing' really meant. We asked them, face-to-face, by e-mail, round the dinner table and at our workshops. Friends, relatives, colleagues, students, correspondents from afar, neighbours from nearby. And their friends. Most had at least been at the receiving end of lectures. Some are involved in giving lectures. A few have been celebrated as National Teaching Fellowship Award holders in the UK. And some have nothing to do with higher education. Our respondents probably represent a relatively normal distribution curve in terms of age, offering a reasonable cross-section of society ranging from 13 to well over 80 years old. The gender balance is not far from equal. All freely gave their thoughts about what the term 'lecturing' brought to the surface of their minds, and allowed us to edit and present their thoughts in this short chapter of our book. All who gave their names are listed on the 'Acknowledgements' page at the front of the book. Several people gave their contributions anonymously, and we thank them too.

In this chapter we present a selection of their responses to our question; for readers who would like yet more such definitions, we've included many more in the Appendix at the end of the book. You will note, however, that many of the responses to our question go much further than just describing lecturing, and address some of the purposes of lectures in general and how to achieve some of the objectives of lecturing.

Lecturing is...

" Lecturing: it may be a word that has lost some of its relevance in education. It carries negative connotations of 'being lectured at' as in 'he or she gave him or her a good lecturing'. This has, to an extent, devalued 'lecturing' as the best word to describe working to facilitate learning within a large group. 'Engagement' of the audience with both deliverer and subject is something to which all 'lecturers' aspire. Finding ways of getting large-group students to interact with each other, to reflect and respond to the material as it is being delivered, is a challenge. As is presenting the traditional 'hour's worth' of material in a way that fits with the students' diminishing attention span created by exposure to other forms of information presentation (TV, video games, etc). "

(UK National Teaching Fellowship winner)

" 1. The stupid haranguing the stupefied.
2. Reproving at length.
3. Oral delivery of a written non-fiction text.
4. Systematic oral instruction in, or exposition of, a subject. "

(A retired professor of literature in Canada)

" For me, in the context of higher education, it's about creating a large-group learning experience. One only learns some things about Beethoven's 8th Symphony by sitting there in the concert hall watching and listening. Less by just listening to recordings (students taping lectures, etc). More by watching and listening along with the score. Even more by talking to people who know more (or less) about it. And so on. Most, I guess by conducting it, and persuading 80 or so professional musicians about what the balance, tempo, tone, volume might be to make it work best. So conductors learn most from the process – as of course do lecturers. But lecturers don't always become sufficiently aware of what they can be learning – and make the same mistakes next time (like some conductors). "

(A professor of educational development)

" Creating a story (with a beginning and an end, and an interesting middle) – some of which is developed by my students. "

(A lecturer in microbiology)

"An anachronistic form of teaching in which the teacher takes all the responsibility for deciding what the students are to learn, for preparing the content and for 'delivering' it – too frequently, badly. A magnificent learning experience for the lecturer (assuming he or she carefully thinks through what is to be taught and digests and organizes it well) and at best of doubtful value to the learner in most respects – and in many instances an insult to the intelligence of students in higher education. "

(A professor from New Zealand)

"My definitions come from a student's perspective of what lecturing appears to be from my point of view. It should be noted that my definitions only come from a direct result of studying for many years at the University of X:

1. The attempt to explain in as much detail as possible, a subject that is either known or familiar, while at all times giving the impression that you know a great deal more.
2. The attempt to explain in as much detail as possible a subject that is unknown and unfamiliar, giving the impression that you are not acting or pretending to know, while at all times hoping that no one has any questions.
3. The attempt to explain in as much detail as time will allow a subject of great importance to participating students in a manner which keeps them awake or at least semi-conscious.
4. The relaying of highly relevant and important information, read the night before.
5. The communication of information between a person qualified to know something and those who are not.
6. The passing on of information outlined in a syllabus regardless of relevance to the subject.
7. A quick and fairly easy way for postgraduate students to make ends meet. "

(A student who recently gained a Master's degree in computing)

"Lecturing is a traditional form of teaching with the primary objective of imparting knowledge to learners about a particular topic. In this respect it is not very effective, though it remains pretty well the ubiquitous strategy in post-secondary education for supplying learners with knowledge and is sufficiently institutionalized to be expected. Effective lecturing recognizes the limitations of this medium and augments the knowledge-supply function with learning texts (eg lecture notes and handouts). It focuses, instead, on those aspects of teaching that can only be delivered face-to-face: inspiring and motivating – making a subject 'come alive' and using performance skills to engage with the subject matter and explain it. "

(Head of a research school in health and social welfare)

"Theoretically it's about passing on information and knowledge to learners to equip them to meet the learning outcomes. In practice (my practice), it's about doing that and developing a questioning and enquiring mind, through scenario, role play, questioning the status quo, analysis and interpretation, considering bias issues, and so on. Mmmm, hadn't thought what it was I did before. "

(A quality manager for a professional body)

"I think it falls into a number of phases:

- identification of a need to communicate a topic or topics;
- preparation for that communication;
- delivery of the communication;
- assessment of how well the communication has been received;
- self-assessment of the delivery of the communication;
- review for the next communication.

This does not explicitly deal with the pastoral implications of lecturing but it can be argued that this fits within the phases identified, eg if communication is to be effective then the recipient must be able to receive the communication which will not be possible if he or she is under stress or there is other noise in the system. "

(A senior lecturer in accountancy, and senior examiner for a related professional body)

"Lecturing is engaging with a large number of people simultaneously to convey such things as information, enthusiasm, knowledge and to generate interest among the audience and participation if you are lucky. "

(An educational developer, experienced in the built environment field)

"Lecturing is a situation and an activity. It can be good or bad:

- **Bad situation:** what passes from the notes of the lecturer to the notes of the student without passing through the minds of either.

- **Good situation:** a mature mind engaging with a large number of maturing minds facing each other in one place.
- **Bad activity:** casting artificial pearls before real swine.
- **Good activity:** it all depends – on purpose, content, discipline, maturity of audience, degree of interactivity, etc, etc – and that is before one has decided whether a political speech (Pericles' funeral oration), a sermon (Jesus on the Mount), a rabble-rouser (Demosthenes' Philippicas) are 'lectures'. **""**

(Senior heroic educational developer and guru)

""Any number of students learning with the teacher at the centre. The teacher sets out the journey, the steps and (largely) the pace, however interactive it becomes. Also, the teacher is seen as the main source of knowledge, wisdom and balance in the session (the teacher has the big picture). I suppose for me, the main point of the lecture (at Level 1) has always been to help students develop this big picture, to be a focus for the contextualizing of all the detail, a framework in which to build the understanding. I suspect that by Level 3, we should be challenging things a lot more, almost using the lecture to help students develop the confidence to deconstruct the framework and build their own... This is probably very variable with subject discipline. **""**

(Educational developer/lecturer)

""Someone talking and a lot of people listening. **""**

(A pre-university learner)

""Rather late on in my career I decided to act on the well-known research evidence about the concentration span of student in lectures and decided never again to give a 50-minute lecture without breaking it up with at least two activities. The challenge over the last dozen or so years has been to devise a range of exercises which engage the students actively and meaningfully in their learning. The term 'lecture' needs to be deconstructed, as the experience of students will vary both within and between lectures. At its most basic it is probably useful to distinguish between 'formal' and 'interactive' lectures, where the distinction is based on the extent to which the students are passively/actively involved in the event. **""**

(UK National Teaching Fellowship winner)

“Like sitting with a colander on one's head: the metal reflects information from the zones of lack of concentration and the perforations allow all manner of thought-provoking snippets through. ”

(A science teacher)

“Actions done by overpaid, out-of-touch, arrogant, middle-class people, living in a world where only education exists. ”

(A student who dropped out of higher education)

“The presentation of information in a didactic manner *or* death by talking head? ”

(A staff developer)

“A means of 'munication (partly mine and partly that of Derek Rowntree). A personal dialectic. A performance, where the lecturer struts and frets and the students tut and stretch. A well-rehearsed act in which the lecturer carefully crafts an analysis of East and West and what may happen next but where, immediately afterwards, the students speak of little else but what happened last in *EastEnders*. ”

(UK National Teaching Fellowship winner)

“Lecturing is an opportunity to air one's own knowledge of the subject in front of a (usually) attentive audience. ”

(A business studies lecturer and musician)

“Lecturing is what parents do to young children, eg our young son recently stole £20 from my wife to buy some Pokémon cards. We lectured him subsequently on stealing! Lecturing is a one-way process whereby learning is achieved by passive listening and observing. Lecturing should have a limited place in university teaching where active and interactive learning are preferable! ”

(UK National Teaching Fellowship winner)

“An interactive learning session, involving a human guide passing on knowledge and stimulating thinking and learning in others. ”

(Geography lecturer)

"A talk by someone barely awake to others profoundly asleep.**"**

(Lecturer in surgery)

"Seeking to convey ideas in a way that to hearers often feels like trying to scale Everest without oxygen.**"**

(A young assistant curate)

"Being told something you don't wish to know, by someone who 'knows' better than you.**"**

(A retired teacher)

"Lecturing is the new word for teaching people too old to be treated as 'kids'.**"**

(A retired schoolmaster)

"A lot of talk to the uninterested.**"**

(A retired postmaster)

"Conveying ideas and information probably not original. Those without pens or pencils maybe absorb more than the 'scribblers'.**"**

(Anon senior citizen)

"A form of posturing in front of people anxious to maintain the illusion they are still awake.**"**

(A young lecturer)

What does this tell us?

The striking thing about these responses is the frequency of strong reactions, both negative and positive. The negative definitions portray a gloomy picture of unhappy and unproductive practice where learning is often almost completely absent from the scene. Those who gave us these powerful reactions spoke with the strength of personal experience, particularly the students represented here. Where positive definitions were provided, these often came with qualifying or modifying statements referring to the purpose, process and practice of lecturing, basically arguing that lecturing can be a good learning opportunity, but only when certain conditions have been satisfied. In other words, asking the question, 'What is lecturing?' actually led many of our respondents to go into the questions, 'Why have lectures?' and, 'What can lecturers do in lectures?' These questions provide us with an agenda for action that we follow in subsequent chapters: how can we make sure that lecturing contributes to rather than diminishing students' growth and development?

3 Histories, philosophies and architecture

In the previous chapter we've spent some time opening up issues relating to lecturing and exploring a range of definitions of lecturing. Here we will look more closely at the historical background of lecturing, touching briefly on learning theories, and then discuss some of the environmental factors which impact on lecturing, factors over which the individual lecturer has little or no control. The link in this chapter between the historical background, theoretical approaches and the physical location of lecturing is inevitable if we wish to deconstruct a series of implications seemingly inherent in the process of lecturing.

Lectures are not new and if we went back into classical times, it is likely that in Greece and Rome we would have seen activity that we would recognize as reasonably close to lecturing. Methods of teaching in the ancient European universities (Paris, Bologna, Oxford and Cambridge) in the late 12th and early 13th centuries included both lection and disputations, where the Master makes a proposition and the Bachelor offers arguments for and against the proposition, with the Master summing up at the end. These disputations followed practices going back to ancient Greece and beyond.

In the lection, the Master would record or speak text that was then copied down by the students. Memorization was one of the areas of activity that were regarded as highly important in the medieval curriculum, and it seems certain that the Masters would have had access to vast amounts of material which they had memorized and which they would then recall in sessions, which would also include disputation and commentary, suggesting that from earliest times, lecturing at its best would involve the students. Extant copies of editions of lecture notes from the 13th century have been discovered, for example, in Paris. In addition, through the Pecia system, handwritten books were reproduced in non-monastic scriptoria run as family businesses producing cheap texts for student use, which were hired out.

Conventional wisdom has it that lecturing developed at a time when handwritten texts were the only kinds of books available, and these were necessarily time-consuming and expensive to produce or reproduce. Hence the necessity for the teacher to read or speak from memory, with students noting or copying down what was said. This methodology has been current for centuries and still offers the benefits of having a live expert in the same room as the learners, with the potential for questions and interactions (although the definitions derived from real-life respondents to our call for definitions of lecturing indicate that this opportunity is commonly an ideal rather than an actuality).

Where a prepared text is delivered (by reading or from memory) as a polished entity, with students recording what they can of the original, or in later times receiving a completed text on paper for future reference, this implies a conceptual model that signifies a master–apprentice approach to teaching, with the pedagogue at the centre of the process taking responsibility for delivering material to the students, rather than a model involving any kind of partnership between teacher and student. Such a model has implications not only for the methodology, but also for what is taught (with an expectation that the lecturer is the principal or only source of information and therefore has a substantial duty to be comprehensive, and at least to take account of the range of known material on the topic). Ramsden (1992, p111) describes this approach from an Australian perspective:

> Many teachers in higher education implicitly or explicitly define the task of teaching undergraduates as the transmission of authoritative content or the demonstration of procedures. The knowledge to be handed on to students at this level (in contrast to the knowledge constituted in research and scholarship at higher levels) is seen as unproblematic. Subject content exists *sui generis*. It must be instilled in students. Much of the folklore of university teaching follows a similar line; even the Robbins Report, subsequently endorsed by the 1987 White Paper, defined key functions of higher education in terms of transmission of culture and instruction in skills. The traditional didactic lecture, of course, is a supreme representation of a perspective on teaching taken from the point of view of the teacher as the source of undistorted information. The mass of students are passive recipients of the wisdom of a single speaker.

Evans (1993) in his influential book about people who teach and learn English at British universities quotes a lecturer from Newcastle (subject unknown) writing in the *Education Guardian* (29 October 1991) for whom lecturing is specifically defined as *not* teaching:

> I am not a teacher. I am not employed as a teacher, and I do not wish to be a teacher. I am employed as a lecturer, and in my naivety I thought that my job was to 'know' my field, contribute to it by research, and to lecture on my specialism. Students attend my lectures but the onus to learn is on them. It is not my job to teach them.

Lecturers with this view of their role are less commonly encountered these days in a world where external scrutiny of teaching frequently demands a recognition of the place of the student in the learning process. In the UK, this is particularly influenced by the activities of the Quality Assurance Agency, which requires the curriculum to be expressed in terms of what students have learnt or can do at the end of a programme rather than what is taught. However, compliance with institutional or national requirements does not necessarily imply a change of mindset, and approaches not dissimilar to that of the Newcastle lecturer quoted above can still be encountered in many higher education institutions today.

As a variant of these models of lecturing from the position of an authority, Fox (1984) in his useful discussion on personal theories of teaching, describes a *shaping theory* which:

> views students or at least student brains as raw material (metal, wood or clay) to be shaped or moulded, or turned to a predetermined and often detailed specification. When (such) teachers are describing their teaching... their favourite verbs are 'produce' (produce a competent engineer, designer, architect) and 'develop' (develop a capacity to solve problems, to manipulate data, to handle equipment...). These teachers also frequently use the language of the athletics coach or the industrial trainer.

This model of shaping learners draws upon the influential and frequently quoted imagery associated with teaching used by Charles Dickens in *Hard Times*, also quoted by Fox (1984), in which he talks about education, not uncritically, in terms of the contemporary industrial revolution: 'He and some one hundred and forty other(s)... had been lately turned at the same time in the same factory, on the same principles like so many pianoforte legs'.

Such premises of lecturing often make use of a positivist view of the world, which bases knowledge on 'rational, logical and empirically verifiable information, with an assumption that there are known and relatively unchangeable truths' that can be passed on to students in their entirety, as Webb (1996) suggests in his powerful text, *Understanding Staff Development*.

In a post-modern world, such certainties cannot universally be assumed. Interestingly, earlier models of knowledge were based on a metaphysical and theological account of the truth. Webb (1996) suggests that we tend to forget that a Platonic view of knowledge was based on a more transitory and changeable world in which:

> We must be therefore careful to distinguish between the naïve impressions of the world which we obtain through the *senses* from essential truths which may only be procured by contemplation through the *mind*... Applying this to teaching, the sensory real world experience we have of a form such as 'the lecture' should not obscure the ideal or perfect form which can be approached through a thoughtful imagination.

We may be coming full circle, then, in that models of thinking influenced by contemporary critical theory may be returning to more discursive and participatory models than those which have predominated in recent centuries. Many today would argue that lectures in which students are passive recipients of a process of information transfer are less helpful than those in which students are actively involved in the construction of knowledge, for example, through discussion. Bligh, in *What's the Point in Discussion* (2000b, pp2–17), makes a powerful argument based on a wide range of research data that discussion methods are more effective than presentations such as lectures in teaching thinking skills, and is effective though perhaps not efficient in teaching information. He suggests that activities that engage students in talking to each other within the lecture room such as buzz groups and pair work make for much more effective learning experiences.

The model of lecturing we are offering in this book has an expectation that students in post-compulsory education have a level of autonomy and need to take responsibility for their own learning. This doesn't let lecturers off the hook in terms of presenting well-researched, up to date and carefully thought through content, but recognizes that they don't have to be the omniscient source of all wisdom that might otherwise be expected. This is a great relief to many of us. If the lecturer is regarded as only one of a range of information sources available to students that also includes books, journals, Web-based material, other students, other staff, their own relevant work and life experiences and so on, then the onus of responsibility is more sensibly shared, we would argue. Lecturing then is not a matter of providing students with knowledge, but more a matter of them constructing knowledge from the range of information sources available (Webb, 1996, pp85–97).

Implied here is also a shift in the power nexus in the movement towards student-centred learning, for example as discussed by Stephen Brookfield in *Understanding and Facilitating Adult Learning* (1986). This Copernican shift from the tutor to the student as being at the centre also makes more possible a deeper engagement by students with their own learning, moving away from surface approaches which Biggs (1987) and others have associated with less successful learning. Traditional lectures, where the expectation is that students copy or take notes as part of a one-way transmission process, seem almost to be designed to encourage surface learning, although this is certainly an over-generalization in the case of those inspirational bravura experiences we recognize as being the products of great minds, immaculate drafting and powerful, passionate presentation techniques, which some of us remember with awe. We would suggest that these are not common occurrences.

Architectures...

However, it is the model of lecturing described above that for the most part underpins the planning and design of lecture theatres in even the most modern buildings, with rare exceptions.

Regarding the new Said Business School at Oxford, designed by Jeremy Dixon and Ed Jones, the *Guardian*'s architecture critic Jonathan Glancey argues that design of form and function come together to recognize the power of the marketplace in student learning:

> The cloister gives way on its east flank to seminar rooms and, on the right, to three highly distinctive lecture rooms. Lined in strips of varnished timber, these are quite unlike the yawn of lecture rooms known to many students. Instead of a dais facing banks or seats, the seats wrap around the lecturer, who, as a result, is forced to interact with students. The students here, mostly postgraduates with an average age of 29, are treated very seriously. As they pay £30,000 per year, this is hardly surprising. (*The Guardian*, G2 section, Architecture, 10 December 2001, p10)

It is disheartening to hear as we did anecdotally from a member of the Building Services staff of a modern university that teams in one part of the organization were busy converting a large flat teaching room into a tiered lecture theatre at exactly the same time as elsewhere on the campus a new tiered lecture theatre was being constructed in a formerly flat room. He wearily suggested that the academics could do well to get their act together and decide what they really wanted to do in classrooms, and it became apparent that the decisions being made by estate management were not including inputs from the teaching and learning committees of the relevant faculties about what models of teaching were priorities for the organization!

In the next section, we look at some of the significant features of the architecture and building services' aspects of lecture theatres that impact on the process of lecturing. Here and elsewhere in the book we also suggest ways of working in unpromising environments, often making the best of a bad job.

The lecture theatre: a place for learning?

the lecturers ...

Professor Oakwood

We are very proud of our historic buildings, but some of the lecture theatres are a bit antiquated. St Margaret's Hall has some very fine old stained glass, but the seating fills what used to be the nave and I think some of the students have difficulty seeing the board properly.

Dr D

It's better now we have cameras, which show on monitors what we are doing on the demonstration bench. But even so, when we're looking at fine-tuning of equipment, it's difficult to show students exactly what you mean.

Arthur

The evening classes have it hardest, especially in the winter. When I show the slides in the warm, dark room, even I feel like falling asleep sometimes. I don't dare sit down when I'm working the projector – it would be so easy to nod off!

Anya Wilenska

Students here complain all the time about the lecture room facilities, but they ought to be grateful. In my country overhead projectors are not commonly used, and we have to re-use transparencies, as they are difficult to replace. They should recognize how lucky they are over here!

---

students' views ...

That lecture theatre is disgusting. Must have been built in the 70s when chocolate brown and avocado were fashionable colours, and never been touched since. There's ancient chewing gum under the seats and graffiti etched into all the benches. It's not what I expected to find at a decent university.

Last in, sit on the steps. Not enough seats for everyone, so if you're not there in good time it's hardly worth going in. It makes it difficult when we have to get across the campus for another lecture.

I'm pregnant, and I thought I was going to faint in the last lecture. It's an airless place at the best of times, and the sun streaming in through those plate-glass windows was unbearable.

I'm not going any more. It's ok if you're in the equivalent of the dress circle, but up in the gods you can't hear, you can't see, and when students get noisy the lecturer just turns a blind eye. It's not a place where I feel I can learn anything!

Lecture rooms around the world are much the same. Some are scruffier than others, some have better or worse audio-visual aids, some provide more comfortable seating and writing environments for students, but in essence all lecture theatres provide a context in which one speaker can address a large group of learners who are there to 'listen, mark and inwardly digest'. Traditionally, lecture rooms provide tiered rows of seats, sometimes in straight rows, sometimes very close in design to the amphitheatres of classical times, with seating curved around and rising from a central dais, platform or podium. In medical, dentistry and veterinary schools, the layout can be designed to allow students to watch actual operations and dissections taking place behind glass, with the lecturer providing a running commentary.

In some instances, particularly more recently, the room is flat with tables rather than ranks of seating theatre style, and a lectern, podium or demonstration bench may form a real or metaphorical function of centring the focus on the presenter. However, the principle remains the same: students sit and receive tuition from a lecturer on whom all eyes are focused, and whom all ears are straining to hear.

A range of factors can impact on how successful the lecture room is in providing an environment in which students can learn. Many lecturers find themselves working in contexts that they regard as far from ideal, with all kinds of extraneous factors over which they have no control impacting on their lecturing. These are discussed below.

Acoustics

Purpose-built lecture theatres are normally designed to be acoustically effective, but this is not always the case in practice. Conversions (from churches, factories, office space, 19th-century army drill halls, and so on) may make imaginative use of interesting architectural spaces, but may be hell to be heard in! Whether the walls are faced with brick, concrete, wood, fibreboard, fabric-covered panels or plaster can impact significantly on the ways in which the lecturer can be heard, and spaces that are designed to be effective for other purposes, for example for musical performances, can be deeply unsatisfactory for lecturing purposes.

Other things that can impact on how well the lecturer is heard include:

- noisy heating or air conditioning;
- noise pollution from nearby roads, factories, performance areas (the Students' Union club nights at one university caused real problems for evening classes taking place in an adjacent building), and other classrooms;
- audio equipment which may be poorly designed for the space, or simply elderly or unreliable.

Visibility factors

Most lecturers make use of some kind of visual aids, and the lecturer can be the most important of these. Factors that impact on how well the lecturer and the visual material used can be seen include:

- poor sight lines caused by pillars and other obstructions, particularly in flat lecture rooms;
- distance from the demonstration bench, dissecting table or operating theatre, making it difficult for students at the back to see the fine detail;
- poor visual aids: scruffy, shiny and superannuated blackboards, whiteboards that have been written upon too often with the wrong kinds of pen, overhead transparencies of text that has been photocopied direct from textbooks in a font that cannot be clearly seen even in the front row, video material or slides with poor focus or resolution;

- where lecture theatres are too big to hold all the students, it is not unknown for overflow rooms with video monitors to be set up to accommodate students who can watch the lecture on a screen in real time.

Comfort factors

Comfort factors that may interfere with student learning include:

- excessive heat or cold that cannot be controlled by the lecturer or students (some institutions still have heating systems run off a central boiler, or have thermostats in different buildings controlling the temperature by computer);
- excessive glare from unscreened windows, which makes the lecture an uncomfortable experience and renders visual aids difficult to see;
- poor-quality air circulation, which can make the atmosphere stuffy and smelly (a lecture theatre in a former radiation laboratory with a sealed air circulation system was known for the ghastly aroma of the (mostly male) students' trainers at the end of a long series of lectures!);
- drab, dismal and dated décor that feels oppressive to lecturer and students alike;
- dirty and litter-strewn lecture rooms: where lecture theatres are timetabled continuously over a 12-hour working day, the last classes are likely to find the room unacceptably messy since servicing and cleaning of rooms is not normally carried out between classes;
- seats may have been designed for students with average-sized physiques only; large or tall students may be uncomfortably cramped, while short or small students may find it really uncomfortable to sit on benches where their feet do not reach the floor and where the work bench is unusable as it is out of reach (the authors of this book recognize one of these problems each!).

Logistical problems

Logistical problems that can make life difficult include:

- lecture rooms with insufficient entrances to enable students to come in or go out quickly;
- tiered seating that is retractable, which is both noisy and unstable;
- lecturing positions located next to entrances so that late students can't enter quietly through the back doors, but need to pass noisily past the lecturer to take up their seats;

- hard flooring, which means late arrivals and people having to leave the lecture part-way through make unacceptably high levels of noise.

Failing to solve logistical problems can have most unpleasant effects. In a 'News in brief' item in the *Times Higher Education Supplement* 'room rage' was reported. The Director of the Modular scheme at a large university in the South West of England sent a memo concerning the change-overs between sessions in the main lecture theatres:

> Following an unfortunate case of 'tutor rage' before the Christmas break, I have been asked to ask you to remind academic colleagues that lectures should finish by 25 minutes past the hour (at the very latest) in order to avoid congestion at change-over times; the large number of students involved now makes this a Health and Safety issue and we must try to avoid stressful situations. (*THES*, 18 January 2002, p13)

So what can we do?

In Chapter 6 on lecturing tools you will find helpful advice on coping in adversity in some of the contexts where you are trying to use some of the technologies of the lecture room in non-ideal places. Figures 3.1–3.6 show some suggested solutions to teaching in difficult rooms.

Meanwhile, here are some more general ideas about overcoming some of the physical problems we've mentioned above.

Making the most of difficult spaces

What you can do in a lecture in terms of encouraging students to interact together as Bligh (2000a) would propose, is to some extent determined by the layout of the room. For example, Cox (1994, p73) suggests:

> It is often easier to get answers in a question-and-answer session, if, at the start of the course, the class is divided into small groups with about five students each. You then direct the question at a particular group, after allowing some time for conferring, one of whose members is obliged to respond – the group decides on the spokesperson. Obviously the type of lecture accommodation and seating arrangement is relevant here and a large flat room with grouped tables is preferable but, failing this, it is not difficult to adapt to a tiered lecture theatre.

However, it is possible to be creative in the use of difficult spaces, and Bligh and others (Brown and Race, 1998; Gibbs *et al*, 1992) provide

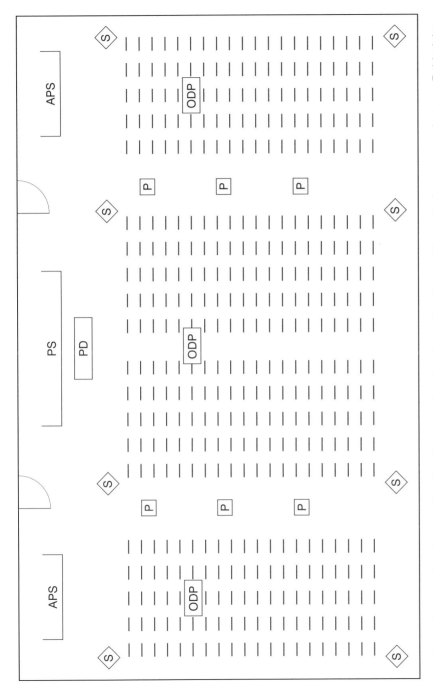

This large, flat room in a former office block at a modern London university provides a challenge to any lecturer. Behind the presenter's desk (PD) at the centre front is a raised projector screen (PS) that students in the centre block of seats can see, but students on either side of the pillars (P) have to look at the auxiliary projector screens (APS), onto which images are projected from the overhead data projector (ODP). A microphone is essential, with sound amplified through speakers (S), but sight lines and audibility in this unpromising room are poor and student concentration in the back rows is weak.

Figure 3.1 Making the most of an unpromising lecture room

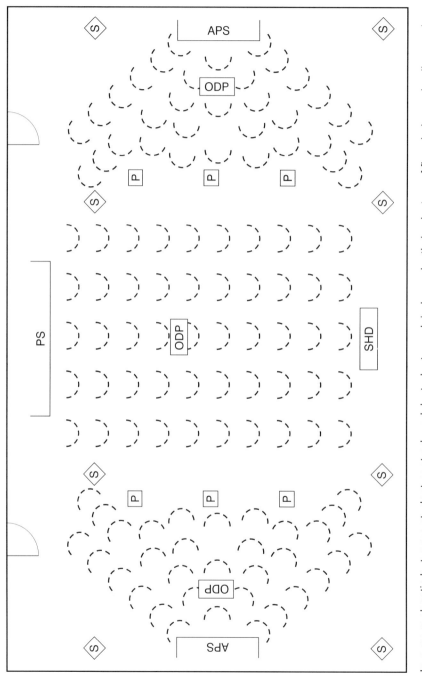

In a more chaotic but more student-centred model, students work independently in clusters of five chairs each, all around the room, with each cluster of chairs facing a screen containing materials that they discuss and work on together. Occasional inputs can be made by the lecturer, based at the staff help desk (SHD), using the three screens simultaneously to transmit short elements of content. The lecturer can also act as a resource when students need to ask questions or seek clarification.

Figure 3.2 An alternative use of an unpromising room

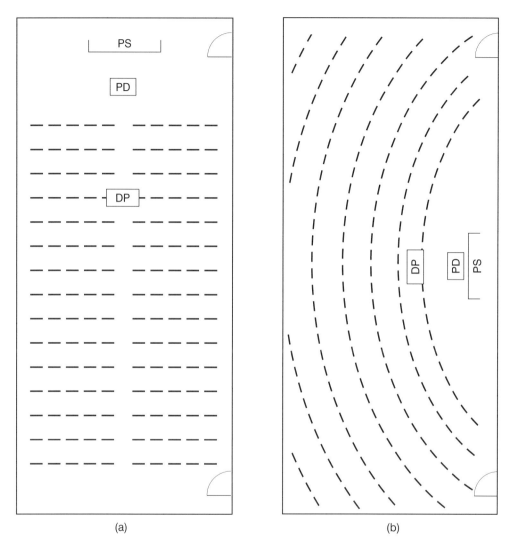

(a)   (b)

In (a) the chairs are arranged in rows along the length of the room, facing the presenter's desk (PD). The presenter uses a floor-standing data projector (DP). The sight lines and audibility at the back are poor, and possibilities of interaction with students after about the eighth row are low. In (b) the presenter's desk (PD) and projector screen (PS) are placed halfway down the side wall, and chairs are arranged in rows curving round the desk. No one is more than 10 rows from the front and interaction between tutor and students is much easier.

Figure 3.3 Using a long, narrow room

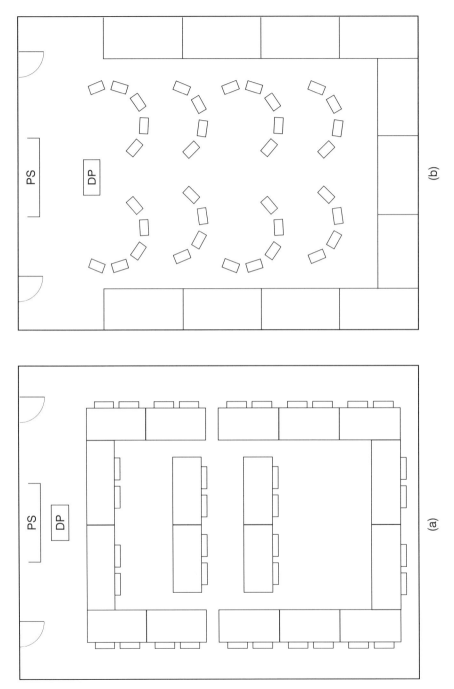

(a)

(b)

In (a) the students are sitting two to a desk, more than half of them facing sideways on to the presenter. In (b) the desks have been moved to the edges of the room and the chairs arranged in less formal 'horseshoe/cabaret style' clusters of fours and fives. This enables students to work in groups facing forward to facilitate discussion and interaction. The downside is that if you then try to lecture formally, students have to rest their papers on their knees!

Figure 3.4 Make yourself unpopular: move the desks

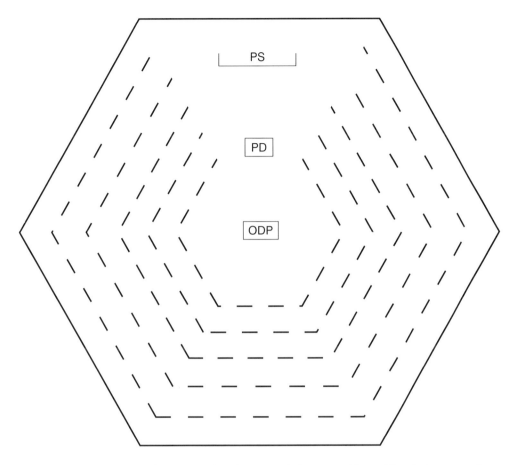

If designing a lecture space from scratch, a hexagonal shape could provide a better arena for learning than more conventional rooms, making it possible for lecturers to interact more effectively with students, and for students to interact with each other.

Figure 3.5 An alternative shape for a large lecture room

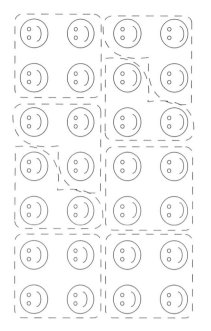

(a)

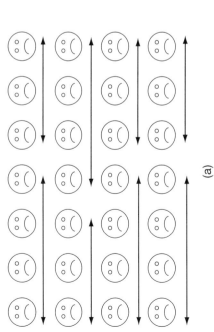

(b)

In (a) students trying to work together in threes and fours along horizontal rows find it difficult to see and hear one another. By asking students to work with students behind and in front of them, threes and fours can happily interact.

Figure 3.6 Getting students working together in a traditional tiered lecture theatre

useful suggestions, with diagrams, indicating how this can be done, working on the principle that students can work in threes and fours in a terraced lecture theatre if they work with students behind or in front of them, rather than trying to make themselves heard by students in the same row.

Addressing acoustical factors

While it is understandable for us to take the view that since we're 'lecturers' we should be expected to be able to muster enough voice power to fill any of the rooms we work in, student feedback soon shows us that audibility is a real problem more often than we might hope. This is often down to room design, and sometimes the students who complain have chosen to sit at the back in any case, but it is still up to us to do what we can to overcome the problem. Among the things we can try are the following:

- Use amplification every time, and agitate for its provision if it is not available. A fixed microphone and loudspeaker system is fairly common in lecture theatres, but is not too difficult to have it installed in other lecture environments where audibility is known to be a problem. A radio microphone is better still, and allows us to move around, for example to get closer to students who are asking questions, and remain audible to the whole group in our responses.
- Don't try to talk all the time in a room where the acoustics are bad. Sometimes we can't have the help of amplification to solve our audibility problems, and need to try our best to project our voices. Even with voice training, it can be tiring to speak quite loudly for any length of time, so it is worth finding ways to limit the time we need to speak by including tasks and activities for students to do at intervals through our lectures, to give us a chance to rest our voices.
- When working in large, flat awkward rooms with bad acoustics (examples known to, and worked in, by us include a former church, a ballroom and an old school gym), you may wish on some occasions to abandon attempts to lecture from the front and instead get students working independently in groups all around the room, with the lecturer taking a position at a 'help desk' in the middle to answer questions, check and chase progress and occasionally to address the whole group while briefing for tasks, taking in responses and coordinating plenary discussion.

Addressing visibility problems

When we know it's going to be difficult for students at the back of a room to see the fine detail of what we might be doing at the front of the room, it is often worth reconsidering what we were intending to show them in the first place. Sometimes it is possible to use additional monitors down the sides of a large room (and some lecture theatres are equipped in this way) so that students can see demonstrations or close-ups of what is going on at the demonstration bench. An alternative can be to put the detail in handouts, as pictures or diagrams, or to use video clips of demonstrations on the intranet so that students can see on their own anything that they may feel they have missed during a lecture-based demonstration.

Sometimes there is no real solution. What worked as a demonstration in a small lecture room with 40 students may simply be impossible to arrange in a lecture theatre with 200 students, and may need to be turned into another kind of demonstration, perhaps as a video clip projected onto the theatre's large screen, or saved for a smaller group demonstration, for example in a laboratory or studio. It really isn't possible to pass round small pictures, books or artefacts within a lecture room and expect students to look at them sensibly in anything other than a small group.

We've made more suggestions about visibility in Chapter 6 on lecturing tools in contexts where projected visual images are being used and the difficulties are caused by the level of illumination.

Addressing comfort and timing problems

These are often connected. Punctuality can be a real problem for students and lecturers alike. Arriving for lectures on time is jeopardized by all sorts of factors, including traffic, finding parking spaces, public transport delays and cancellations, and weather. Even once on campus, it is well known that it can take half an hour to walk through crowded corridors on a route that would only take 10 minutes when the campus is quiet. Students and staff often have to walk significant distances between one lecture and the next, and where one lecture is due to finish at 10.55 and the next to start at 11.05, for example, it is really quite difficult to be punctual for the second lecture, especially if a visit to the facilities is necessary and there's a queue. Some institutions try scheduling lectures at 09.00, 10.30, 12.00 and so on, to give a gap of about half-an-hour between lectures, but with high demand on teaching spaces this sensible practice is not often an affordable solution to punctuality problems.

What can *we* do about punctuality? It certainly helps to lead by example. If we're often late, students get the wrong message, and those students kept waiting by us are not best pleased! It is easy for us to be delayed on our way to a lecture, people stopping us in corridors, the phone ringing just as we're about to set off, and so on, but we need to be firm at such times and make our priorities clear. The other end of the picture is entirely down to us – it's our job to make sure we finish on time. Indeed, it's no great problem when we finish a lecture five or 10 minutes ahead of time – students don't lodge complaints about not getting value for money when a lecture reaches a sensible stopping place a little early, and we bring it to a well-rounded conclusion.

There's less we can do directly about comfort factors. Some lecture rooms have seats or chairs that are really uncomfortable to sit in for even an hour, and it's not unknown for the same group of students to be timetabled in the same room for a whole or half day at a time. In such circumstances, we can reduce the discomfort by having at least some activities where students move around to get into clusters or buzz groups. Even just turning round and talking to the people in the row behind is a change of activity, and allows some movement. In sessions of more than a single hour period, giving students a break can be well worth the time lost. Though it is difficult to get students out and back in less than, say, 20 minutes, the increased energy can mean that we actually save more learning time than we lose. Even in a packed lecture theatre, with some students sitting uncomfortably on the steps, a three-minute 'stretch, chat and shuffle' break can be really welcome to students (and of course can give us a chance to reflect on what's been happening, and come in with a new idea here and there based on what we've noticed from students' body language or questions so far in the session).

A further way to address problems of comfort and punctuality is to enlist students' support in working out solutions. Even when there is little that can be done about the comfort factors, the fact that we've acknowledged students' views, and try to take their suggestions on board can mean that students put up with the status quo more willingly. When punctuality has been discussed with students, and ground rules that take into account their ideas and suggestions have been set, they can feel more sense of ownership of the matter, and may try harder to turn up on time.

When all else fails

Most lecturers can quickly respond to the question, 'Where's your least favourite teaching environment, and why?' What else can we do? It is sometimes possible to arrange a timetable exchange. Someone else might actually prefer to use the tiered lecture theatre between 10.00 and 11.00, and let us use the large flat room for that session where we really want to get students doing some group activities. Someone else indeed may be desperate to use the technology available only in the lecture theatre, and might be only too delighted to swap.

Although departmental and institutional timetables may have few visible gaps in the booking for popular teaching spaces, there are often times when a theatre or room may actually be empty, because the class is out on field work, an independent study element, or an activity based in the learning resources centre. Many institutions do an occasional 'use of rooms audit' and check whether all the timetabled slots are actually being used. Sometimes a large theatre will have been booked for what was expected to be a large class, but actually turned out to be a group that would have fitted comfortably into a smaller teaching room. When there is a climate of flexibility about room bookings, and a way of putting back into the system rooms which become available again from time to time (and we recognize that this is not always the case!), it allows at least some degree of responsiveness to some of the comfort problems mentioned above, even if this is just achieved by an element of variety.

It can be quite useful to become part of the process by which teaching spaces are allocated. If you volunteer to be a member of the faculty or departmental committee which looks after such issues, at least you'll know what the overall constraints are, and you might have a rather better chance of making sure that the particular needs of your own classes are discussed.

Conclusion

In this chapter we've been primarily concerned with the physical aspects of the teaching–learning environment in which lectures take place. This can be perfect – but only rarely. For most of us, at most times, we can see how it could be better. The next chapters in our book look more at what we can do in the teaching environments we actually end up with, and how best we can use them to help our students to get the most they can out of them, even when things on the physical side are loaded against effective learning.

4 Why have lectures?

In the previous chapter we explored the origins of lecturing as a method of teaching in universities. Despite all the concerns that are expressed about the method, lecturing is likely to remain a central part of the higher education scene for the foreseeable future in just about every context except distance learning. But why should we continue to do it? What can we hope to achieve through lectures? What, to echo Bligh (2000a), is the use of lectures? In this chapter we'll look at the rationales that are offered (with caveats) for their continuing use, consider a number of purposes for lectures, and then explore the implications of these for practice. First, using the characters you've been introduced to earlier, we'll consider some of the reasons that lecturers give for why they lecture.

the lecturers ...

Professor Oakwood

Lectures are my chance to interest and enthuse the students, so that those who want to take the subject further can be identified, and I can get to know who they are. However, with classes as large as they are now, there are only a few students in each class who are likely to go on to research in my subject. It's a problem what to do with all the rest. They don't seem prepared to put in the work these days.

Dr Arbuthnott

I love it! I really feel at my best in front of a group of students. I like to feel that I do a good job, give a polished performance and use a wide range of up-to-date media. I put a huge amount of energy into giving the students lectures that are state of the art in terms of delivery.

Bill

I'd prefer not to have to give lectures, but I'm appointed as a lecturer, so I guess it's what I'm expected to do. My teaching timetable is mapped out in terms of lectures, tutorials and practicals. I feel I do better in the tutorials and practicals as I can really talk to the students, but they are supposed to follow on from the things that have been covered in lectures, so someone's got to do the lectures, and I guess it's me when it comes to my specialist topics.

Arthur

I wouldn't do it this way if it were my choice. Since the numbers on the course doubled, it's the only way that the course leader can manage to fit in all the tuition hours they need. They just don't have access to studio space in the way they did in the past. So it's bums on seats really.

Anya

Why lecture? I think lectures are really important. It's the opportunity for the expert to share expertise with the students. In lectures I can tell them what the subject is really about, and what the latest advances are. It's the way to help students to understand the state of the art of the subject. I base my lectures on my advanced research in the field and ensure that I include the most up-to-date references from around the world, so they don't just get a parochial view of the topic. Some of them find it hard though, as there's a lot to take in.

Marisa

Of course lectures are important. It's my chance to bring the subject to life. I can pick up what's just happened, and share it with the students and discuss it, debate it, argue about it, and get them really thinking. The only problems are the shackles that they put on me these days – it's as if lectures were supposed to be set in stone and formulated weeks in advance, and take no notice of what's happening.

Colleagues who have used these case studies in workshops on lecturing have told us that they think they are a fairly typical range of reasons that fellow lecturers give for using lectures. Also recognizable are the range of students' opinions on what lectures are for, set out below.

students' views ...

I go to lectures to find out what I'm supposed to learn. I go to find out what parts of which textbook I should concentrate on, and which articles to get from the library or download from the Web.

I go to find out about the assessment that will follow. Watching and listening to the lecturer is my best chance of finding out how academics' minds work. I need my degree, and don't want to miss any chance of making sure that I get it.

I attend because I really enjoy them. It's great being in the same room as the famous expert, and it's also great to have the chance to compare my views with those of the other people who are there.

I go to lectures because that way I feel I'm on top of my learning. Put it the other way: when I miss a lecture, I feel disadvantaged. True I can copy someone else's notes and photocopy the handout stuff, but it's not the same when I've not actually been there. I don't feel the same about it if I haven't made my own notes as well. Even though there are some lectures where I don't feel I've learnt anything, I tend to go to them all just in case I might miss something that's important.

I'm quite selective. I go to those lectures that I feel are doing me good, and stay away from those where I can't see that I've got anything useful from them. I catch up on hand-outs and notes from such lectures, but use the content to find my own material from books and articles on the reading lists.

I suppose I'm a bit of a conformist. I go to lectures because I guess I'm expected to be there. Even though I mightn't be missed, I don't like to take any risks. I don't want to be noticed in the wrong sort of way.

I go to lectures because if I don't I feel that I'm not studying properly. Sometimes I get a lot out of them, other times hardly anything. To be honest though, even in the boring ones, it's easier sitting there feeling conscientious at being there, than going through the textbook on my own and trying to learn it myself!

It's not uncommon for lecturers and students to have completely different views of what lectures are for and this can lead to all kind of problems of unsatisfied expectations and misapprehensions. It's no wonder therefore that negative feedback can sometimes come as a great surprise to the lecturer who is doing a great job on his or her own terms, but who is sadly off course from the students' points of view. Next then, drawing on the literature in the field we will discuss the value and purposes of lectures.

What really is the use of lectures?

Many writers have taken issue with the use of lectures at all, seeing them as an inefficient means of promoting student learning. For example, Laurillard (1993, pp108–9) argues:

> Why aren't lectures scrapped as a teaching method? If we forget the eight hundred years of university tradition that legitimizes them, and imagine starting afresh with the problem of how best to get a large percentage of the population to understand difficult and complex ideas, I doubt that lectures will immediately spring to mind as the obvious solution. Their success depends upon the lecturer knowing the capabilities of the students very well, and on the students having very similar capabilities and prior knowledge. Lectures were defensible perhaps in the old university systems of selection of students on the basis of standardized entrance examinations, but more open access and modular courses make it most unlikely that a class of students will be sufficiently similar in background and capabilities to make lectures workable as a principal teaching method. The economic pressures forcing open access also dictate larger classes, yet open access makes those teaching methods hopelessly inefficient.
>
> Academics will always define the value of the 'inspirational' lecture as though this could clinch the argument. But how many inspirational lectures could you reasonably give in a week? How many could a student reasonably absorb? Inspirational lectures are likely to be occasional events. Academics as 'students' typically think little of the method. It is commonplace to observe that the only valuable parts of an academic conference are the informal sessions. For the individual learner, the lecture is a grossly inefficient way of engaging with academic knowledge. For the institution it is very convenient, and so it survives.

It seems probable that at least a proportion of students are equally vehement in their rejection of lecturing as an appropriate tool for learning. A student quoted by Evans (1993, p56) talks about it as being 'the most boring medium ever devised. The lecture's been pointless since the invention of printing'. However, many argue, as does a lecturer in a former polytechnic again quoted by Evans, that lectures are what students expect and may even demand: 'They want the lectures. It's the format they've been used to… They would prefer to sit and be lectured to' (p57). He goes on to quote a former head of department at a Northern redbrick university as saying that he thought the department had lost faith in lecturing 'and yet we are going to do more and more of it because we won't be able to cope with the numbers except by lecturing' (p55). This is quite a frequent comment in the literature and in conversations and workshops we have held on lecturing. Despite the advent of electronic means of delivery which are readily available in most countries, lecturing is still seen by many as the most cost-effective means of delivering content in higher education. This has led to its yet wider adoption in many cases, as Gibbs *et al* (1992) discovered in the PCFC-funded 'Teaching More Students' project, even in subjects where it has not been traditionally used to any extent (such as fine art) and where lecturers may remain unconvinced of its relevance or value.

Others have argued that lectures per se are not the problem, but how they are undertaken:

> Despite the firmness of the lecture's foothold, the best general advice to the teacher who wants to improve his or her lecturing is still 'Don't lecture'... Many objectives can be achieved more efficiently and effectively by variations on traditional methods or new methods altogether. This is true for large groups of 100 or more as well as for smaller ones. The task the lecturer faces in both cases is paradoxically how to make 'lecturing' less like a lecture (passive, rigid, routine knowledge transmission) and more like an active communication between teacher and students. In other words, we should be thinking about teaching rather than lecturing. Lecturers ought to provide very clear signals to help students appreciate the links and points of separation between parts of the content, and to enable them to disentangle principles from examples. They should explain what they are doing and why. Talk should pass *between* teacher and students, not from teacher to students. Students should have to do something more energetic than just listening and note-taking, preferably in cooperation with each other, and they should be required to work with the content as soon as possible after the class. There should be opportunities for the teacher to monitor the effects of his or her instruction on student learning in order to see whether students are understanding. (Ramsden, 1992, p167)

He sees a significant part of the problem as being the way in which lectures are used as a means to deliver content in an overloaded curriculum, which in turn is likely to lead to poor or superficial learning (Ramsden, 1992, p71). He also presents as problematic the poor structuring of information within an individual lecture or between lectures and in some cases the lack of any intention to make the material attractive to students. He quotes a medical student interviewed as part of his research who seems to have experienced both the rough and the smooth:

> All too often the lecture or series of lectures would present a string of unrelated points with no structure. These lectures were full of details which were both boring and soon forgotten and they did not make clear what the major points were that we had to understand. To make things worse, many of the lectures seemed to be made deliberately uninteresting, as if the lecturers did not care about whether we understood or not, as if they wanted to show how ignorant and stupid students were... I guess they proved their point with many of them. The... course was just the opposite – the lecturer bothered about whether we learned, and was around to help, and commented on ideas, and I worked a lot harder at this subject. And I definitely will be able to use what I learned as it still stands out so clearly. (Ramsden, 1992, pp76–7)

This view of lecturing is not universal, however, and there are many proponents of the method who champion lecturing as a means of delivering the curriculum. Unlike Ramsden, Cox (1994, p59) would argue that lectures can achieve all the objectives that other methods can, so long as there is clarity about why the method is being used and what it can and cannot do:

> It is currently fashionable to criticize the formal lecture method as being inappropriate in the modern learning environment, when so many other methods are available, such as computer-assisted learning, active learning and open learning. Some authors claim that formal lecturing is only appropriate for certain objectives (conveying knowledge, facilitating comprehension), but not for others (applications, analysis and synthesis, evaluation and criticism). I believe that a properly designed and delivered lecture can achieve all of these objectives. Put bluntly, a lecture can achieve anything that can be done by talking to someone. Of course, it cannot perfect the students' skills – only their *activity* can do that and that is the purpose of the tutorials and their private work. Most teachers have never had any doubt about the function and limitations of lectures. Lectures are only there to lay the foundations, show the way, ease the passage, as the student works through the subject.

At its best a lecture can be a life-enhancing and highly memorable experience, and expert lecturers can provide powerful learning opportunities, as McKeachie (1994, p53) suggests: 'Effective lecturers combine the talents of scholar, writer, producer, comedian, showman and teacher in ways that contribute to student learning.' McKeachie gives a number of other positive reasons for using lectures:

> Lectures are particularly appropriate for helping students get up-to-date information on current research and theories relevant to topics they are studying. Moreover, lecturers may sometimes usefully summarize material scattered over a variety of printed sources, thus providing a more efficient method of conveying information than if students were to be assigned to cover these sources by their own reading. Finally, a lecturer can adapt material to the background and interests of a particular audience – material which in printed form is at a level or in a style not well suited to a particular class...
>
> Lectures also can provide structures to help students read more effectively. In fact the lecture may help students learn to read. Readability of material depends on the expectations brought to material by the reader. Thus, appropriate lectures can build structures and expectations that help students read material in the given subject-matter area more effectively. Many lectures have important motivational functions. By helping students become aware of a problem, of conflicting points of view, or of challenges to ideas they have previously taken for granted, the lecturer can stimulate interest in further learning in an area. Moreover, the lecturer's own attitudes and enthusiasm have an important effect upon student motivation. Research on student ratings of teaching as well as on student learning indicates that the enthusiasm of the lecturer is an important factor in effecting student learning and motivation. Not only is the lecturer a model in terms of motivation and curiosity, the lecturer also models ways of approaching problems, portraying a scholar in action in ways that are difficult for other media or methods of instruction to achieve. (p54)
>
> Becoming conscious of what is going on in the students' heads as we talk, being alert to feedback from students through their facial expressions, nonverbal behaviour, or oral comments, adjusting one's strategies in reference to these cues – these will help the lecturer learn and help students to learn from the lecturer more effectively. (p70)

Lectures continue to be a popular means of engendering passion for a subject, despite the fact that they have fallen out of fashion in some areas. The format of illustrated content delivery is still popular in other media because it can bring content to life in a way that no other medium can. Television history programmes, for example, make use of the lecture format, albeit with outstanding visuals. Contrary to expectations sometimes, this medium can bring in viewers in their millions. The Simon Schama *History of Britain* series shown in the UK on BBC2 Television in 2000–01 had to fight for its place in television history, the idea originally having been put down by a TV executive who shouted, 'Simon, we don't *do* lectures!' But they did, and 3.3 million viewers enjoyed a magnificently illustrated narrative from the TV historian who acted as a viewers' companion to a millennium of sometimes perceived dry history (Willis, 2001).

Opinion continues to be divided in academia, however, and most institutions of higher education still organize high proportions of their teaching around lectures and other classes in which formal presentations are the main method used. In any case, it is indisputable that lectures are here to stay for the foreseeable future:

> Some temerity is necessary for anyone who would enter the conflict between the proponents and the detractors of lecturing. It is hardly an overstatement to say that lecturing remains the pre-eminent method of teaching in most subjects in on-campus institutions. The majority of university teachers seem to favour it; many timetables are organized around it; lecturers will argue that students, especially first year students, are unable to learn without it; most students arrange their studying lives around lectures, and are indeed dependent on it (in some courses it is impossible to determine the content to be learned unless one attends lectures); numerous books have attempted to justify it, to improve it, to change it. Arguments against lecturing are likely to meet the same withering replies that other arguments which cut across tradition in higher education meet: it is not realistic to abandon or even substantially to modify it; it is not economical to change it; it might reduce standards if we tampered with it. (Ramsden, 1992, p153)

This being the case, in the next section we explore some of the reasons why many of us continue to lecture and examine what implications these personal purposes will have on how we go about undertaking the task.

Rationales for lectures

Marris, quoted in Gibbs (1998b), argues that:

> The essential function of lectures is to place knowledge in a meaningful context. By his synthesis of different points of view, or textbook treatments; by his emphasis on essentials, and the extrapolation of basic principles; by the clarity with which he relates the parts of his exposition, a lecturer can enable the student to perceive the subject coherently. But, perhaps even more usefully, he can provide a more personal

context, showing why the subject interests and excites him, how he has used it in his own experience, how it relates to problems whose importance his audience already understands. From this, the student can more easily imagine how he himself could use it: he develops his own context of motives for mastering a problem.

Bligh (2000a) offers the principal reasons for giving lectures as being to:

- aid memory during the lecture;
- aid revision;
- see the developing structure of a topic;
- relate and reorganize during further study;
- select what is important;
- know what has to be learnt; and
- maintain attention.

There are many different reasons cited why we use lecturing as a medium, some carefully thought through and some more instrumental, as the lecturers' views above suggest. In the next part of this chapter we explore 15 of the reasons that have been expounded by participants in our workshops as to why lecturers lecture, the implications thereof, practical issues that arise and some suggestions about how best to go about the task.

Why lecture…?

1. So that we can enthuse our students

This is often mentioned as a justification for having large-group lectures and available research seems to back this up. After all, on such occasions we can aim to get to just about *all* of the cohort, not just the few we may be trying to enthuse in a seminar or tutorial or practical class. At best, we can enhance students' desire to learn. We can help them to go away eager to read more, practise more, try out what they have learnt, test themselves out on what they have understood, talk to each other and continue to learn, and so on. We can also use large-group occasions to clarify to students what they *need* to learn. We can share details of what they will need to be able to do to *prove* to us (and more important, to themselves) that their learning has indeed been successful. We can illustrate the sorts of evidence of successful learning that we have in our minds, as designers of the assessment instruments and processes that will be used to determine whether their learning has been successful.

But what about the students who aren't there? We can't enthuse them. What if they're not there *because* they're not enthused? There's not much we can do about their problem in lectures without them. And what about the students who *are* there, but who give us every indication that they remain unenthused? And what about the students who *are* there, but whose level of enthusiasm is hidden by blank expressions and inscrutability? How can we know what is really going on? We've got to look for more than engaged body language and probing questions from students to gauge their levels of enthusiasm, so that we can strive to increase these levels.

But how *can we use lectures to enthuse students?*

Knowledge is power, and it really helps to know how students are responding to your material. Towards the end of this book we make some suggestions about obtaining and learning from student feedback as a means of improving our lectures. You may consider it worthwhile to build in to your feedback methodology (whether using questionnaires, shows of hands, informal one-to-one feedback, group feedback or other means) some questions specifically designed to gauge how you come across in terms of enthusiasm.

It's difficult to project energy and excitement about a topic if you don't feel it, especially if you have taught the topic many times before, if you feel you have been lumbered with teaching the least interesting areas of the course material, or if you have had a new topic landed on you at short notice, which you've had to mug up at the last minute. But it's worth remembering that for the students, this is likely to be the first time and that issues of course management are not their fault.

Try to put yourself in the students' shoes and think about the kinds of things that are likely to be viewed by them as indicators of your own lack of enthusiasm. Using obviously dog-eared notes, dated or scruffy visual aids, being late, looking unprepared, using a monotonous voice, sounding bored with the material yourself, gazing into distant space and looking as if you can't wait to get away at the end are all things that are likely to be turn-offs for the students.

2. To give the students the information they need

Lectures can be useful occasions to give students information, but it may not be a particularly efficient means of doing so (Bligh, 2000a). The amount of information available on a given topic is now so enormous, that it's impossible for students to write down everything you want to get across to them on a topic, especially within the timescale of the normal one-hour lecture period. In terms of curriculum delivery, it doesn't make sense to use the time available for students to just write down what you say or present. Students are usually keen to get a good set of notes from a lecture, but this doesn't necessarily mean that they have to use all the time available in a lecture writing down what you say.

So how *can information transfer be maximized in lectures?*

It is possible to give them handout materials covering 10 times what they could have written in an hour, so consider how you can combine speaking, getting them to read material within the lecture and other activities (see Chapter 7). It's also possible to make the material available to them in other ways: course manuals, notes that can be downloaded from the intranet, and so on. But if the information can be got without actually coming to the lecture, students may vote with their feet and not come – unless they're getting much more than just information by coming to the lecture. For this reason, you will probably want to balance an element of information delivery with other activities designed to make them think, as suggested above (Bligh, 2000a; McKeachie, 1994; Ramsden, 1992).

3. To cover the syllabus

It is easy for lecturers to be concerned that they're not going to get through the entire syllabus, especially as time goes by. Bank Holidays cause Monday lectures to be missed repeatedly, and other factors reduce the available hours to get through it all. But can lecturers *ever* get through all of the syllabus? And what does 'getting through' actually mean? It would be a rather limited and inadequate body of knowledge that could be completely covered in a mere lecture course. And even if the *information* could be covered in the lecture course that's not the same as engendering the relevant *knowledge* in the minds of all of the students.

So how can we cover the syllabus meaningfully?

More important than mere coverage is providing time to reflect and digest. If lectures are still going on just days prior to exams, it does not give students time to get to grips with the material covered. Some would suggest with good reason that nothing new should be covered after two-thirds of the way through the lecture course. Perhaps the last third should be used to help students to make sense of what they had already started on. But if there were nothing new in the next week's lecture, how many students would turn up? We are left with the need to make that lecture well worth turning up for.

4. To help students to gain a sense of identity

It can be lonely in a crowd. Even in a large-group lecture, there can be lonely students. But they could have been a lot lonelier in their own study-bedrooms or flats, or in a library or learning resource centre. At least in lectures there is the chance that even the lonely students may talk to other students, and possibly make some sort of bond with the lecturer too. Administratively and statistically, each student is part of a group. Funding is based on how many students are in the group. Resources follow student numbers. While we should never forget that a lecture theatre is full of individuals, not clones, it is useful for the group to be together as a whole group for at least some of the time. But of course, those students who repeatedly don't turn up for lectures can't ever use them to gain this sense of identity.

How can we use lectures to encourage cohort cohesion?

Students won't feel part of a community of learning if they don't talk to each other and find out, to however small an extent, how others are thinking. In many cases, seminars, practicals, tutorials, studio work, labs and other task-oriented activities provide opportunities for interaction with groups of peers, but the only place where they are likely to be part of the whole cohort on conventional courses is within the lecture theatre. You might want therefore from time to time to ask for a show of hands in response to questions, or ask them to take part in buzz groups leading to a collective response, or use some of the electronic individual response hardware available in some well-endowed universities to gain a view of how the cohort as a whole is thinking and then share it with them publicly. This need not take up more than a minute or two, but can be reassuring and encouraging for those who might otherwise feel very isolated.

5. Because it's a cost-effective means of curriculum delivery

Compared to small-group teaching, lecturing is cheap: one lecturer can teach hundreds or even thousands of students at a time (numbers vary from country to country; some of the classes considered large in the UK would be regarded as cosy and intimate elsewhere). The economics look good and it's not difficult to scale sessions up when numbers increase, since all you then need is a bigger room (or some more chairs at the back, or sitting room on the steps, or standing room only for latecomers) and maybe a microphone for those with quiet voices. It is not uncommon for audio-visual equipment to stay the same, even though visibility may be compromised for those at the peripheries. This cost-effectiveness is something of a myth, however, if we start to look at learning rather than teaching. Gibbs *et al* (1992) argued convincingly that student performance tends to diminish as class sizes increase and that strenuous efforts need to be made to ensure that more does not mean worse.

How can big (group teaching) be beautiful?

Learning does not have to suffer if group sizes in lectures are large, but it takes more planning and forethought to keep active learning happening. For example, while throwing out questions to the group works reasonably well in a small lecture group, in a large group individuals are likely to feel intimidated about responding and will usually be inaudible unless a roving mike is used. Asking students questions may need to be done in a more structured way, for example by saying, 'Could you all please write down three features you would recognize in Fauvist paintings and then compare them with each other in pairs, before I ask for five volunteers to call out their responses?' This is less exposing than picking on individuals at random to answer a question directed uniquely at them, since everyone will have had a chance to think of an answer and check it with someone else before speaking aloud, and you can watch for people who make eye contact with you to choose as volunteers. It's also a way of preventing confident and articulate individuals from hogging the airtime in question sessions.

Similarly, rather than asking at the end of your lecture if anyone has any questions (normally a signal for everyone to gather together their papers and make a bolt for the door) you could ask them to write questions for you on slips of paper for you to collect, evaluate and prepare a response to, either at the start of the next lecture or on the course bulletin board.

6. As a means of accounting for class contact time – to quantify it

We're in an age of accountability and external scrutiny. The teaching role can be quantified in terms of bums-on-seats x hours-sitting-there. At least that's what people seem to think. There's endless talk about teaching quality, but not enough about learning quality. It's what's happening in the minds-on-seats that's important really. But that's not easy to measure. So we go back to crude measures such as numbers. There is a danger that those looking for practical alternatives to curriculum delivery via the traditional lecture (including the provision of independent study materials) find themselves lumbered with additional class contact hours by managers who see empty lecture rooms and academics working quietly on their computers in their offices and fail to work out what is really going on.

How can we get away from measuring crude class contact hours?

There is no alternative than to encourage colleagues and managers to recognize that promoting student learning in the 21st century can be undertaken by a variety of means that includes (but isn't exclusively) face-to-face contact. It may take some time to get this radical view recognized!

7. To keep track of the students

This is about attendance. But attendance means more than one thing – there's 'being there' and 'being attentive' for a start. While it's relatively easy to measure 'being there', it's much harder to measure how attentive students are. (It is also possible for skilful and determined students to outwit lecturers' attempts to keep an accurate register.) Nevertheless, falling attendance at lectures does give useful messages, both about the lecturers and about the students. Falling attendance leads to something being done about it, sooner or later. But falling attentiveness may not be acted upon until too late (or may not even be noticed at all!)

How can we check attendance and attentiveness?

Taking conventional registers in large groups has never been an effective means of doing this and has provided endless opportunities for impersonation by friends, 'hilarious' sobriquets and outright falsification. Electronic swipe cards (with photos) to be swiped at the lecture room entrance are used in some institutions, but unless there is a genuine reason for confirming attendance (eg employers' requirements for confirmation of day release students' attendance), you may wish to abandon attempts to police physical presence and consider instead ways of making the lectures unmissable!

Checking attentiveness is harder. Students who *look* attentive can be miles away in their minds. But it is much easier to gauge students' attentiveness if they're doing things (intentionally) from time to time during the lecture, and we'll return to the agenda of what we can cause students to do during our lectures in Chapter 7.

8. Because we like giving lectures!

Many lecturers find giving lectures the most rewarding aspect of the role. At its best, a lecture provides you the chance to share your experience and expertise, to get excited about the things you are really interested in, to work your way through a reasoned argument of a complex set of contradictions in a logical and coherent manner, to put a novel spin on a well known set of issues and to energize and galvanize your students to go out and take the topic further.

However, there are undoubtedly some lecturers who like hearing themselves speak and enjoy the power trip of showing off their expertise and wisdom before a large group of people with less experience and knowledge. Some lecturers are supreme *raconteurs* with a huge repertoire of occasionally relevant but largely unrelated anecdotes, jokes and personal experiences that they weave effortlessly into a narrative that the students enjoy hugely. For them, the performance is the thing, and while these lectures are likely to be memorable to students in terms of the experience, they may remember little of the content being expounded after the event.

At least, it can be argued, the people who *like* giving lectures are not likely to be accused of lack of enthusiasm, and probably will give their lectures with some degree of confidence, passion and conviction – both of which are important for the students in their audiences. But we will argue later in this book that the act of *lecturing* in itself is not the be-all and end-all of making lectures cause students to learn. Once again, we return to the central focus of this book: *facilitating student learning* in lectures.

But how can I know that my enthusiasm is contagious?

How do I know if the students regard me as a bore, a figure of fun or worst of all, an entertaining and self-indulgent idiot? Ask them! (But perhaps not in those precise terms!) You will probably be able to tell from their verbal and non-verbal cues if they find your lectures fun (celebrate if they do!) but you may wish to go deeper than this. Ensure that the student feedback mechanism you use differentiates between whether the students find your lecture enjoyable or a valuable means of learning (of course we always hope it will be both). Take note of what it tells you and, if necessary, modify your lecture style accordingly.

9. To help students to map the curriculum

This is in many ways the overarching purpose of lectures. Students need ways to find out *what* is most important for them to learn, *why* this is so, and *how best* to go about their learning. The lecture content of a course is often taken as the *must know* agenda, and may be thought of as sufficient to pass forthcoming assessments (but not to excel in them). Lecturers bring to the occasion the benefits of tone of voice, a range of examples, topical allusions and other means of bringing the topic to life. Lecturers can also prompt and answer questions, along with many other factors that aid the process of helping students to focus their learning and structure it in the overall context of their studies.

How can I know that the map is working for students?

Students often respond positively to lecturers who clearly signpost how a particular lecture fits into the programme/unit/module and who help them to evaluate the relative importance of different elements of the material. This can be usefully undertaken in a scoping lecture at the beginning of the course of lectures, which helps to provide a frame of reference for the material that follows and that gives guidance on what activities the students need to engage in within and alongside the lectures (including, for example, note-making, using handouts productively, wider reading, using course bulletin boards and electronic discussions, making use of related practical sessions and so on).

However, lectures are not the only means of mapping the curriculum. Distance learning students may never attend a lecture, but still achieve qualifications. The course documentation, expressed in terms of intended learning outcomes and related assessment criteria, is an alternative way of demonstrating the scope and extent of the curriculum, whether for conventional students or distance learners. One way or another, the curriculum needs to be further developed and demonstrated in different ways by recommended textbooks, journal articles and paper-based and electronic resources.

10. So that students can estimate how they are doing

We don't need to worry much about making sure that the high-fliers know that they are high-fliers. They will show their qualities through assessments. But by definition, high-fliers are a minority. Many of the rest of the students in a large-group lecture are concerned, to a greater or lesser extent, with how their studies are going. Though there are some students who don't care much about their progress, for whatever reason, most students do want to be successful in their studies. In a lecture, they have a shared experience with the rest of their class, and can pick up quite a lot to help them work out how they are doing.

How can students gauge their personal progress?

Students can detect cues from the body language of others sitting around them. They can check out whether the questions that a few students may ask are questions they themselves have been thinking about. When something puzzles them, they can at least see whether other people there are being puzzled about the same things, or ask fellow-students who don't seem puzzled for explanations. Again, of course, those students who are habitual absentees can drift far away from any feedback on how their learning is actually going – even if it is going well enough.

11. So we can estimate how our students are doing

Lectures can be useful for this. We will find out sooner or later how our students are *really* doing, perhaps through their assessed course-work, and later still through summative assessments such as exams. But by then it may be too late: some students will have failed. We are necessarily more concerned about student retention than ever before, not just because high rates of drop-out are a negative performance indicator for any external scrutiny of quality our institution may be subject to, but also because student failure in higher education has a huge cost to the students themselves, their families and others who invest in their education. In lectures, we get some general cues to how students' learning is going, although it is difficult to pick up on individual performance within a large group. The cues we get from students can be helpful in general terms and can help us to anticipate problems before they become insurmountable.

How can we know?

Their questions give us useful indicators. The expressions on their faces can help us to tell whether they are understanding things. That is, of course, provided that our students don't become too skilled at *looking* as though all is well in their learning when it isn't! That's where building in some means of checking students' understanding of key concepts and ideas within the lecture can be invaluable.

12. So that students' feelings and attitudes can be changed or developed

This can be one of the strongest justifications for having large-group lectures, although Bligh (2000a) indicates that changing students' attitudes should not normally be the major objective of a lecture, since lectures aren't usually particularly effective at doing so. Inevitably, it depends on both the ability of the lecturer to argue a view cogently and convincingly as well as the willingness of students to accept the possibilities of viewpoints other than their own.

How can we use lectures to challenge preconceptions and provide competing views?

Lectures *can* be pivotal shared experiences where students' assumptions can be challenged, and where the lecturer's own attitudes and feelings can be presented as one of a number of alternative views, allowing them to probe their own responses and reactions. Providing the opportunity for students to hear and consider the variety of views held by recognized authorities within the field that compete with the lecturer's own, as well as those held by other students within the cohort in the lecture theatre can be enormously powerful, but if handled badly, may leave students confused and bewildered.

13. To help students learn how to turn information into knowledge

We keep returning to the theme that information isn't knowledge. If students just go out from lectures and file the information contained in their handouts, however neatly, they still haven't turned it into knowledge. Students need to *do* things with the information before it becomes their knowledge. The information they've been given will of course already be *other people's* knowledge, not least that of the lecturer giving it out. Images of curriculum delivery that use the metaphor of the postal service ('Here's a really handy parcel of data to you from me') rather than the labour ward ('We can help you when you get into problems, give you advice when you get stuck, help to ameliorate the pain of the process, intervene when things get tricky and support you in all kinds of ways, but in the end, you have to do what no one else can do for you') are unhelpful. We have (or should have) moved well beyond Gradgrind's view of teaching in Dickens' *Hard Times* of lots of 'little vessels... arranged in order, ready to have imperial gallons of facts poured into them until they were full to the brim'.

How can we get students to turn information into knowledge during lectures?

Students may need to be (sometimes reluctantly) prompted, encouraged and pushed to move out of a passive recipient mode of learning into a more active one. Research cited above suggests that it's only when the students have applied, extended, compared, evaluated, argued with, summarized, contested and played around with the information they have been offered and have linked it to their own existing knowledge base, that it becomes *their* knowledge. In a lecture, however active, there are likely to be limited opportunities to help this to happen, but we can give students indications of what we expect them to do with the material both in the classroom and beyond to help them to internalize the concepts in useful ways, rather than just absorbing it.

14. To help students to learn how to learn

'Surely not!' lecturers sometimes say to us. 'They should have learnt that long before we see them. After all, they're *proved* that they know how to learn in the qualifications that got them to university in the first place.' Such views miss out on one important thing – we *all* need to continue to learn how to learn throughout our lives and careers. *What* we learn gets more complex. *How* we learn it effectively becomes more crucial. The techniques that are likely to get students admitted to university in the first place can quickly become out of date and inadequate as the demands on them increase. In particular, there's a lot of consensus these days about the need to help students to become progressively more autonomous as learners as a course progresses, but this is likely to make tried and tested study skills that worked in the early stages less valuable as the educational outcomes expected of the student become more complex. Autonomy in learning doesn't just happen, however, except perhaps for the highly able few. For most students, the path towards becoming autonomous learners is quite a rough one and they are likely to need guidance on how to achieve this goal.

How can we help students to become more autonomous in lectures?

We can't *make* them become better at managing their own learning – only they can achieve this. But we can use the shared learning experiences of lectures to throw some light on *how* they can go about gaining ownership and control of their approaches to learning by giving them specific advice on their own metalearning. Many lecturers feel reluctant to divert any of the lecture time away from delivery of the content outlined in the course programme and towards helping students think about how they are learning. But Entwistle (1998) and others argue that learners who consciously examine their own approaches to learning tend to be more effective and deeper learners, so it is worth making some space in the programme, even if only in short but productive bursts, to ask them to be reflective. If we can help them to bring to the surface of their thinking matters of *how* they learn, and can encourage them to share with each other their approaches, and to gain from each others' triumphs and disasters, they are likely ultimately to become more productive learners.

15. To help students to tune in to our assessment culture

We've already thought about how *learning* becomes more challenging as students progress from school to university, and then through the various levels leading to their degrees. Equally, the assessment culture in which students have to demonstrate the products of their learning continues to develop. Unlike school, at university in the UK it is normally the lecturers themselves who design the assessment instruments and processes which students will face. Therefore, lectures can provide occasions where students can tune in to how lecturers' minds work, and thereby become better at estimating the nature and scope of the assessments they will face, and the standards expected of them by their different assessors.

Much is said (Entwistle, 1998) about students becoming more strategic as the proportion of the population involved in higher education increases and competing pressures are exerted on students' time. It can however be argued that being strategic about assessment is an intelligent response to the situation students find themselves in.

How can we use lectures to guide, without spoon-feeding?

If we as lecturers can use our lectures to accommodate students' thirst for cues and clues about the standards expected of them, it can only help them to fine-tune their learning so that they get credit for it in due course. This is not entirely without self-interest on our part. If our students do well in their assessed work, we are deemed to have done well in our lectures. This can bring with it the danger that we try to make sure that our students do well by spoon-feeding them. Indeed, colleagues whose students do less well may charge us with having done so. There is therefore a fine balance to be struck between allowing students to tune in to our assessment *culture* and telling them too much about what will be involved in the assessment *menu*.

Reasons enough for lectures?

Some of the reasons we have explored above are more powerful than others, but most of them have at least something going for them when we address them directly in our lectures. Essentially, we would not have committed ourselves to writing this book if we were not convinced that lectures are here to stay for some time to come, and that they are well worth doing, if done well. There is a lot to recommend them! Notice that we said 'lectures', and not 'lecturing': there is much more to designing a lecture than just standing there lecturing.

We need to ensure that this method of fostering students' learning is 'fit-for-purpose' in that it is based on a clearly thought through rationale, it is undertaken effectively, efficiently, in a way that is appropriate for the context and the student cohort and that, in the jargon, it does what it says on the tin!

In this chapter we've looked at a variety of reasons for lecturing, addressing the issue of *why* before we move on to considering *how* in subsequent pages. In so doing we will first discuss what you as a lecturer can do in lectures to make lecturing a powerful tool to promote student learning and what tools you have available to make a good job of it. After that, we will look at what students can do for themselves to maximize the usefulness of the experience.

5 What can *you* do in your lectures?

This chapter aims to explore what lecturers can do in lectures. Not just how we can lecture, rather how we can survive from the moment we walk in to the lecture theatre to the moment we leave. We'll be exploring in more depth in Chapter 7 what *students* can do, but clearly we need to bring the student presence into the present chapter straightaway, as the whole purpose of lectures needs to include the aim that students should get useful learning payoff from being there.

We'll look at our actions in lectures in two stages. First there are our behaviours, including how we make ourselves heard, and attempt not to betray any nervousness we may be experiencing. Then we'll get down to the more significant agenda of how we use our words as we lecture, with a particular emphasis on how our approaches impact on student learning.

Lecturers' views

Ask most lecturers about what they *do* in lecture rooms, and the answers tend to be about the *effects* of what they do, rather than the actions that are the causes of these effects. Let's look again at some of the fictional characters we presented as vignettes at the start of this book and think of a few of the things that are found in the wide range of perspectives which lecturers bring to their approach to preparing and giving lectures.

the lecturers ...

Professor Oakwood

Over the years I have built up a really good set of notes that I deliver with a new spin year on year. I suppose they are getting rather scruffy now, but I like to use them as my base material every time and extemporize around my main themes. Of course there's always new things to say, so the difficulty is sometimes fitting it in within the hour. I feel as if I'm giving them their money's worth though.

Bill

I work really hard to get on top of the content and I'm really happy about what I'm telling them. I find the actual process of lecturing more of a strain. Sometimes I like to use the good old whiteboard to work them through a problem, and they seem to really like that, but it's always really embarrassing if I make a mistake, so I've tended to do that less often recently. It's less nerve-racking to have it all pre-prepared.

Arthur

What I like to do is give the students a chance to see a range of images and start making connections. Sometimes I put in a startling or disconcerting image to see how they react and sometimes it works and sometimes it doesn't. You can never quite tell how they are going to react, but that's the whole point really. It's supposed to be challenging and even experimental sometimes.

Marisa

I had this woman in watching me teach last semester as part of our quality review. She wanted to know what I was going to do with the students in the session. What a stupid question! What does anyone in my subject area do in a lecture? We give them the material that they need to pass the professional body exams. When the chips are down, there's this mass of content they've just got to master, and in lectures I work my socks off to make sure that they are in a position to do so. Nothing special about that.

You might recognize some of these traits in our fictional lecturers. They (we) are all trying to do a good job in the lecture theatre, sometimes without thinking through the effects of some of their actions on the students' learning. Let's now turn to some student perspectives.

students' views ...

Have you seen those notes! They must be 20 years old, yellowing, dusty, curled up at the edges and covered in that tiny spidery script in several different colours. We are running ourselves into debt for the rest of our lives to be here and I think we deserve better than that!

Nice guy and all that, but he really suffers, and I can't imagine why he puts himself through all that stress. I quite like it when he shows us how he works through the kind of question we are going to have to do in the exam, but it's awful when he gets it wrong. I had to help him out last time actually and point out where he had made an error. It made me feel quite good, but we shouldn't have to be doing that.

I appreciate the way that he brings in stuff from all the latest journals. It makes you feel as if you are getting all the cutting-edge material.

I find it a bit daunting trying to cope with all the different conflicting points. I prefer really to have one perspective to concentrate on, though it's quite interesting some-times, the way she tells us something and then the next minute gives us a completely different point of view.

He's really weird! He'll be in the middle of one topic and then from nowhere throws in this completely off-message stuff. He's not rambling, but I can't follow his thinking. Perhaps he used a lot of drugs in the 60s when he obviously bought all his clothes and it's affected his thought processes!

I find him really sexist. We can be in the middle of a lecture on contemporary painting and then he'll chuck in a slide of a Renaissance nude. What's that supposed to be about? I find it disconcerting and rather unacceptable.

You feel as if you are in a sausage machine. The content gets churned out, week by week, and you just sit there and take in what you can and make a good set of notes so you can learn them for the exams. It feels like a very sterile process, although she does her best to give cases where she can to illustrate the concepts and make it memorable.

Of course, these students' views are just the tip of the iceberg. If we ask students what they *like* about what we do in our lectures we will get a much happier story. But it's responding to the things that students find difficult about our lecture-room performances that can bring the richest harvest of information to help us improve our lecturing. What we do in our lectures has profound effects on students' learning experiences. Our actions can put students right off our subject – or switch them on to go and research much more about the ground we have covered in a lecture. Perhaps the real problem is that we're not always aware of what we are doing in lectures, or of the effects our actions are having on students at the time.

Actions speak louder than words?

Let's start our analysis of what you can do in lectures by addressing some of the most common problems that lecturers encounter – nerves, nightmares and drying up. Then in the second part of this chapter we'll look at the business of *choosing* the words that will help the lecture to be a satisfying and productive learning experience for the students.

Stage fright

Lecturers who happen to have been trained to give public performances are at an advantage – but are relatively few. Some can bring to their rescue techniques learnt through past experience in amateur dramatics, after-dinner speaking or even pantomimes. For most people though, at least at first, the sight of a large roomful of students watching expectantly is enough to produce at least some symptoms of anxiety, such as sweating palms, rapid breathing, and strange distortions to the sound one's voice makes when one tries to use it confidently! Standing at the front with a roomful of students looking at you can make you very self-conscious. Some new to the job are made so nervous by the experience that they stand transfixed on the podium, barely moving a muscle. Others look as if they are auditioning for jobs as bookies' runners or on the floor of the stock exchange, and still others find nervous mannerisms not formerly apparent, such as pacing like a caged tiger, surfacing in the lecture theatre.

Students can be very cruel and tend to caricature any behaviour they view as odd. They are also fairly forthcoming in advising you of their observations, and this can only increase any original nervousness.

Everyone needs to find a public persona that feels natural to them. Lecturing is a bit like being on a stage in a theatre, where normal-scale movements tend to be invisible. How much you use illustrative gesture probably depends on how outgoing a person you are, but you may wish to scale up your hand and arm movements for effect. Watch others whose lecturing style you admire and see what they do. If you are feeling brave, watch a videotape of yourself in action with the sound turned off and see how you look. It is hard at first to avoid self-consciousness, but again this is a matter of time and personal comfort levels. Avoiding gestures completely will make you look wooden and stiff to your students.

Building your confidence

There are no quick fixes that will get you through the nervousness that many lecturers feel at the outset.

In many contexts, excellent preparation is the best antidote to lack of confidence, so the work you do prior to the lecture is likely to make you feel more comfortable. In addition, you might like to try some of the following:

- Make sure you know exactly what you are going to say right at the beginning so that you are not lost for words when you start. Write them down if it helps, but try not to look at them other than in extremis.
- Take a couple of deep breaths before you start to speak (without overdoing it) as it is often the first few words that sound a bit squeaky.
- Make sure you have a drink of water on hand so that if you get a coughing fit or your throat feels dry, you have something on hand to help. Many lecturers also find that a sip of water buys thinking time when a student asks a complex question to which they don't want to give an instant answer.
- Make sure you can read your own notes and don't be too vain to wear glasses if you need them. Use a really big font size so that you can see at a glance what you have written, and number the pages so you can reorder them if they get mixed up.
- Watch other people whose lecturing style you admire, and try to analyse what it is that they do well so that you can emulate it, so long as it fits in with your own personal style.
- Get someone to watch you teach and ask them in the early stages only to comment on what you do well.

Starting the lecture

We don't have a second chance to make a good *first* impression. Therefore at the start of the lecture, we need to be seen to start off the occasion in a firm and definite way. This is sometimes less under our control than we might wish, with latecomers straggling in. In this respect, we're between a rock and a hard place. If we wait till everyone has arrived, those who have been in their seats for several minutes feel unrewarded for their promptness. If we start prematurely, the latecomers may miss the important starting stage of any lecture, when we explain what the particular occasion is about, where it fits into the bigger picture of a series of lectures, and how it follows on from the agenda of our previous lecture.

Managing time and structure in lectures is often about making compromises. We can sometimes accommodate the effects of latecomers by building in a short but interesting 'prelude' stage at the beginning of our lectures which, although interesting to those present, is not in fact crucial to those who have not yet arrived.

Time flies when we're enjoying ourselves. Perhaps the biggest danger that most lecturers face in their lecture-room time management is that 50 minutes can go by so quickly. A nominal one-hour lecture should never exceed 50 minutes in practice, as it usually takes at least five minutes each way for a student class to get in and out of the theatre or lecture room. When things go wrong with our time management, everyone notices – the students, the class waiting to get into the venue and (not least) their lecturer, eager as we ourselves are to get off to an unflustered start.

When a skilled lecturer manages time and content flawlessly in a lecture, no one actually notices. The processes don't interfere with the content. More importantly, students' confidence and trust levels are linked (strongly, and often subconsciously) with our own apparent confidence and control of our techniques in the lecture room. It is when time and content trip us up that our actions are really noticed by students – and indeed by anyone else who happens to be observing or monitoring our lecture-room performance.

Dressed for the occasion?

Being up there in the limelight with all eyes focused on you means that what you wear is of more significance than it is in the seminar room or the practical class. The habit of wearing an academic gown for lecturing has mostly died out, but it solved a lot of problems when it was in currency. In some institutions and some disciplines there is an expectation that lecturers be dressed relatively formally, for example in a suit. In other places, to dress in this way would inspire ridicule. Explore what is normal practice where you work and then find out what version feels right for you. If you are already feeling nervous, you don't want to wear anything too tight or constricting, and powerful lights and the press of hundreds of students can make the lecture room very hot, so be sure to think ahead about coping with high temperatures. Figure-hugging or revealing attire may get you the kind of attention you might not wish to attract and may be offensive to some of your students, so is probably best avoided.

Being heard!

If you talk to new lecturing staff, one of their most frequent worries is about whether they can be heard properly in lectures. The commonest industrial injury reported by people working in education is serious damage to their voice, caused by strain.

On any observation checklist about lecturers' behaviours on stage, audibility is present as an indicator. Once you've learnt to overcome nervousness, there's a lot you can do to address making yourself heard. For a start, it's worth accepting that very few lecture halls have been designed for optimum audibility, and you will usually need to do quite a bit of fine-tuning so that your voice is rendered audible in each different lecture room you encounter.

Many lecture rooms provide microphones and other means to amplify your voice; this is usually a good solution, since it takes a lot of the worry out of the situation. Problems may arise if the mike is fixed to one spot, which may make it difficult for you to interact naturally with your students. Nowadays many rooms have in-built sound systems or there are technicians who can supply a radio mike on request, which means you can move about more easily. Normally with a radio mike there is a pack you put in your pocket or attach to your belt, with a clip-on mike that you need to fix just below your larynx on a lapel or tie. If you know you will be using a mike on any day, it's a good idea to think about what you are wearing, as the clips do not sit well on a plain round-necked jumper or blouse. On the top of the pack there is usually a slider that you need to remember to turn on (a red flashing light usually indicates that you are live) and do remember to turn it off when you stop. Once you are wired for sound, you need to check that the receptor unit is switched on and working.

Whether you are using voice amplification or not, it's a really good idea to go into any new lecture theatre in which you will be teaching in advance of your first session there, so that you can check out the technology and how your voice sounds. It is less frightening to do this than walking cold into a new room full of students all waiting for you to start.

Most people do not find it easy or natural to talk to large numbers of people in a big room without shouting and straining their voices. Individuals need to find out what works best for them, but many people find some kind of voice training very helpful. What you need to learn to do is to project your voice better, rather than just speak louder, which can strain vocal chords. This is largely achieved by improving breath control. Most people need to stand up to lecture if their voice is to carry to the back of the room. The chest cavity should be open, so shoulders shouldn't be hunched, nor should you stand stiffly to attention. When practising, look at an imaginary person in the middle of the back row (or take a friend with you to give feedback in the early days) and speak to that person, so you know what you are aiming at.

When you are speaking to a class, you will project more effectively if you are looking at the students, so this makes speaking audibly and reading aloud from notes pretty much incompatible. In classical times, academics would memorize what they wanted to say and nowadays politicians have autocues, but neither of these options is really viable for jobbing academics with full timetables, so you will need to find your own way around this.

It is usually beneficial to speak slightly slower than you would do in a one-to-one situation, and to articulate just a little more clearly. This means moving your mouth parts used in voice production (lips, tongue, teeth and palate) a bit more than you would normally do (without taking it to ridiculous extremes). Practise at home in front of a mirror and look at what your mouth is doing. If you can barely see your mouth moving at all when you speak normally, the chances are that you need to articulate more strongly when you are lecturing. It's all a matter of practice and gets easier the more you do it.

Think about the pitch of your voice and notice how it changes when you talk in public. Women's voices often rise in pitch when they are nervous, and the pitch of men's voices can drop to a low rumble in times of stress. You may wish to emulate the tactics (if not the practices) of well-known politicians and media figures, who consciously moderate the pitch of their voice to make them seem more authoritative and serious when speaking in public.

It usually helps to take a slightly deeper breath than when speaking at normal volume (without hyperventilating) and to concentrate on directing your voice to the furthest point in the room. The volume should be increased to some extent, but if you feel any exertion or soreness in your throat, this means that you are straining your voice and you should stop doing it! However, most people can train themselves or be trained to project well enough in medium to large rooms with good acoustics to cope without trauma. Often it's a matter of confidence as much as physical factors. If you feel you are struggling even after following these suggestions, seek some further advice from a voice specialist.

Getting through the syllabus

Lecturers often wistfully explain that one of their biggest problems is that they don't feel they get enough time to get through the syllabus in their lectures. Even with the best planning, there are Bank Holiday Mondays, Student Union meetings, bad weather, travel problems, and the entirely unforeseen attack of flu.

A rather robust response to them could be, 'But *you* don't have to get through the syllabus; it's *your students* who need to get through it. You've passed your exams, you've already got through it. It's their turn now.'

Most syllabi seem to have grown as subject knowledge has expanded. It is hardly ever the case that there is really time in a series of lectures for the lecturer to 'take' the students on a guided tour of the entire syllabus. It is perhaps best to regard a series of lectures as 'spotlights', identifying the really important issues. These are often the most difficult ones for students to understand well, and are worth the time spent treating them in depth in lectures. Spotlighting can be much better for students than 'emulsion painting' – trying to spread out all the syllabus thinly onto all of the students!

Of course, when deciding what will *not* be included in our spotlighted lectures, we have to be really clear that it *is* included in students' syllabus content. For example, we can use part of our lecture time with students to include carefully formulated *briefings* about what they are required to do under their own steam, which sources to select from, and (above all) how to check out their learning of these parts of the syllabus so that they find out for themselves how ready they are for the related questions that will be included in their end-of-module exams. If students are quite clear that (say) 60 per cent of their marks will relate to what is addressed in lectures, and that the other 40 per cent is entirely dependent upon their own independent (or collaborative) work on the rest of the syllabus, most students rise well to handling the responsibility for the work beyond the lecture programme.

It remains useful to ensure that there are clear opportunities for students who encounter difficulties with the 'uncovered' syllabus areas to benefit from question-and-answer sessions or problem-solving surgeries, scheduled at appropriate times alongside the lecture course.

Losing the plot

Let's assume now that one way or another you've cracked the issue of audibility, and are in control of your voice and nerves. Once they've got started speaking, many people's remaining nightmare is that they'll dry up.

It happens to us all at one time or another. It is sometimes the case that we're so busy explaining something, and trying to gauge whether the students are following us, that we completely forget what we're going to move on to next. Even in normal speech, it is not uncommon for people to just draw a blank occasionally.

Perhaps the first thing we should remind ourselves when confronting these fears is the old adage, 'silence is golden'. There is absolutely nothing wrong with a short episode of silence when we've finished one important point and are about to move on to another. Furthermore, what seems to us to be a *long* silence is likely to be regarded by students as a much shorter one – or perhaps not noticed at all, as they quietly reflect on that last important point and finish making any notes about it.

However, we do indeed need to have our route-map through the lecture. That doesn't mean we have to follow it slavishly – especially when important questions arise from students, or when we have a useful idea for a topical or relevant tangent that seems just right for a spontaneous addition to the occasion.

It can be really useful to bring in to any lecture a couple of short, optional tasks for students to do, right there in the lecture, should time allow. For example, 'I'd like you all to just pause for a minute or two to identify what for you are the most important areas we have covered so far today, before we continue with the next section'. It's especially valuable if we can put up a task briefing for one of these, at hardly any notice, on a prepared overhead or slide. With PowerPoint, these can be 'hidden' action buttons that can be triggered as or when we decide to use them (see how to do this in the next chapter). The extra minute or two gained while the students get on with the task can be lifesaving for us, as we rediscover exactly where we are on our route-map.

It is also useful to design our route-maps flexibly in the first place. Some of our slides, and indeed some of our spiel can be optional. It makes a much better impression on our students that we don't appear rushed or flustered if there are elements of our lecture agenda that we don't actually manage to get round to in a particular lecture. Students only notice what we do – they don't know what we decided not to do, nor do they need to know if it was optional in the first place.

Some professional speakers produce cue cards (often using 5 × 7 inch index cards held together with a treasury tag; ask your parents what these are if you're under 30), with their key points encapsulated on them. Others find it helpful to use bullet points on overhead transparencies or in a PowerPoint presentation as a prompt for what they have to say, but of course this means you will have to speak to your notes rather than follow a carefully pre-prepared script. (For more detail about using technology and visual aids in the lecture room, see the next chapter.)

Adding 'finish' to your lectures

Students are keenly aware of the progress of the clock during most lectures. Unless we've got them spellbound (a rare luxury!), they are the first to notice the minute hand of the clock approaching five-to-the-hour. It seems entirely natural to students that by about 10-to-the-hour we should be at least beginning to wind up the lecture. We should be heading for a natural stopping place, summing up, going back to the particular purposes of the lecture, or some such appropriate closure phase of the event. If, however, we are so absorbed with what we are saying, or indeed with answering students' questions, to the extent that we run out of time, the last impression is of not being in control of our actions.

There are often things we would have wished to have said, that it is best not to try to say in the time left to us. We can make a note to address the most important of these matters in the next lecture, as we move into our wind-up stages promptly and hopefully seamlessly. There is no second chance to make a good *last* impression.

Making our words work

This is, of course, what we've been leading up to in this chapter. One way or another, the expectation is that when we're giving a lecture, we'll be talking for at least some of the time. That's why the issue of audibility needed to be addressed first. But even if we've got the voice of a film star, the authoritative tone of a guru and the presence of a great leader, we've still got to decide how best to use our words.

For a start, speaking well is a different art to that of writing well. We're still talking about words, but a long sentence in a scholarly article doesn't always communicate itself best by being heard. Besides, long sentences are difficult in lectures because we run out of breath!

So what do we *do* with our words in our lectures? There are several possibilities. For example we can:

- read them out from our script to the students;
- put them on screen from overheads or PowerPoint slides;
- put them into students' hands directly, in handouts open before their eyes.

Perhaps the first rule of 'making words work' should be not to try to do more than one of the above at the same time! Students can read faster than we can talk. If the words are already on-screen, students quickly become irritated if we read out to them words which they can already see. It is much better for us to indicate (with a pencil on the transparency, a cursor on the PowerPoint bullet point, or a red spot from the laser pointer – if, of course, our hands are steady enough so that the red spot does not do a tango on the screen!) *which* words we are referring to, and then to *explain* them further, or *expand* upon them, or *argue* against them – and so on. The same applies to words that are already in our handouts. Of course, it is important to consider the possibility of students having visual or reading impairments that make it difficult for them to read directly from the screen or page, so it may be worth checking this out in advance. (See Chapter 10 on taking into account students' special needs.)

So, how can we make optimum use of our words in our lectures? Let's confine ourselves, for the moment, to the words we say. There are many different ways we can use words orally. These include:

- reading them out from our script;
- reading them out from a source (book, article, newspaper, learned treatise, manual, etc);
- reciting them from memory;
- dictating them to our students, so that they write them down verbatim;
- speaking them spontaneously off the top of our heads;
- describing things to students;
- elaborating on a cue or prompt in our script;
- asking a question;
- answering our own question;
- responding to a student's answer to a question we've asked;
- responding to the puzzled look on the face of a student in the fourth row;
- bringing together the strands arising from several students' answers to a question we've asked;
- suggesting to students what they should do with the idea we've just expounded;

- briefing students to argue with each other for a minute or two about which of two options might be the better one to choose, and why;
- telling a story to set the scene for a task which students are about to try;
- gaining attention by offering an anecdote; and so on.

In short, there are many more things we can do with words in our lectures than simply read them out to the students. Moreover, just reading our words out to the students is probably the least profound use we can make of words in our lectures, except perhaps when we want to quote literally using other people's words.

Next, what about our students' learning payoff? We want students to be *learning* as a result of the words we say in our lectures. We want to get them thinking. So what controls over student learning have we got at our disposal, in the words we choose to *say* in our lectures, over and above the words we choose to show on-screen or in handouts? There are several things, including:

- tone of voice – accenting the really important words;
- body language gestures – providing additional emphasis where we wish;
- speed of delivery – helping students to distinguish key ideas from background information;
- facial expression – telling yet more about the meaning of the words we say;
- repetition – providing cues to the relative importance of particular words or phrases;
- pitch, volume and all the other controls on our voices;
- audible and visual evidence of our own passion and enthusiasm for the topic of the lecture.

All of these skilfully combined represent powerful benefits in terms of student learning, and contribute to a sound rationale for having large groups of students sitting in lecture theatres for a shared learning experience.

So how can we make best use of the words we say, to optimize our students' thinking and learning, at any moment in the middle of our lecture? Let's explore some of the ways we can use the spoken word in our lectures, thinking now particularly of what we want to be going on in our students' minds as we speak them. Of course, for most lecturers, words are only part of their side of giving a lecture. There are also diagrams, pictures, video clips, sketches, flowcharts, sound-bites, and other illustrations to be considered. We'll look at these in detail in the next chapter. Meanwhile, let's consider just a few of the ways we can use words in our lectures, in terms of the learning payoff in our students' minds.

Dictating

While this is certainly one way to fill up a 50-minute lecture, it's not known for being efficient as far as learning payoff is concerned. It used to be a sensible thing to do when books were rare and expensive, and before the invention of photocopying and offset litho printing. Nowadays, if our prime intention is that students have their own copies of particular words, especially extended tracts of words, life is too short just to dictate to students.

For students' with dyslexia and/or whose first language is not English, dictation can be a huge trial. Furthermore, students know very well that it is possible to write down dictated words quite quickly, efficiently and accurately without ever *thinking* about the meaning of the words!

Reading your words out from your screen or script

If the only effect of reading out extracts from our notes, books, articles and sources is that students attempt to copy down the words (or even summarize them), the learning payoff is little greater than when students are dictated to. But we're trapped between two stools here. If the students already have the words in their handouts, and we read them out aloud, they are likely to switch off in terms of reception – after all, they've already got the words. However, if we're doing something more than just reading them out, it might be better.

Explaining things to students

This often works best when the students already have the words and we're not reading out the same words to them, but using different words to explain what is meant by the words they've already got. Now it might be argued that the explanations could also have been pre-prepared and included in the words on the handouts that students already have. But then, we'd have lost the chance to use the power of tone of voice, emphasis, body language and so on to help students to *make sense* of the words they already have. We'd have lost the chance to help students to *make* notes, rather than passively *take* notes.

Explaining things to students works best when they already *want* to know what something means. Therefore, it can be useful to prepare students to want to find out the answers to questions by using our words in lectures to set students up with questions in their minds.

Asking questions

It has been said that the '?' is the most important character on the keyboard. A question mark implies that some thinking needs to be done. At the simplest, is the answer 'yes' or 'no'. There are several common bases for questions, including:

- Who?
- What?
- When?
- Where?

There are also interrogatives, which are often more important, including:

- Why?
- Why not?
- How?
- How else?
- What else?
- With what?
- With whom?
- From where?
- What's the difference between... and?

Then there's the even broader (and sometimes most important question-starter of all): so what?

It can be said that 'everything important is simply the answer to an important question'. If we take this viewpoint on board, it can be argued that students' receptivity during a lecture is likely to be much enhanced if the words that are used by the lecturer alternately *ask* important questions, then proceed to *answer* them. But of course there will be many questions to which students already have an answer, or at least a view, so why not ask them the questions and let them take ownership of the best answers? Asking questions, in our view, is a way of using words in lectures that can promote high learning payoff.

Towards a teaching taxonomy?

Back in 1956, the work of Bloom *et al* set off the momentum to describe learning in terms of what students could *do* when they'd successfully learnt something, including cognitive, affective and psychomotor actions. A hierarchical taxonomy of verbs was developed, as an attempt to quantify the learning that took place during a wide range of teaching or training scenarios. This in turn led to working out the objectives for teaching events such as lectures, or to use the current term, 'intended learning outcomes'. In this chapter we've been exploring the other side of the equation – what *we* do in our lectures, especially those actions that are intended to cause students to learn. It can be really productive to try to work out a sort of 'teaching taxonomy'. In other words, which of the many things that *we* do in our lectures have the most significant effects in terms of students' learning? And in the context of this chapter, which of the ways in which we use spoken words in our lectures have the most significant payoff in our students' minds?

So far, we've explored in some detail only a few of our speech-related actions, in terms of the learning that they may cause in the lecture room, without even digressing into all the further learning we intend our students to achieve using print-based resources such as textbooks and journal articles, and electronic resources such as the Internet, our local intranet, and all the computer-based resources and databases in our institutions. We've gone back to the basics of what we can aim to have happening *in situ* in our lectures, to fuel the fire of all the subsequent learning we may hope or intend to happen.

There are many, many more ways of using words in lectures than reading, explaining and so on, discussed above. You might like to think of how *you* learnt your own subject, and what processes worked best for you as a learner. You may then think back to those whose teaching influenced you most, and reflect on *how* these teachers used spoken words to best effect in their teaching.

Further ways we can use words in our lectures include:

Arguing	Motivating	Prioritizing
Proving	Challenging	Inferring
Contextualizing	Parenthesizing	Distinguishing
Conceptualizing	Discussing	Solving
Confirming	Comparing	Deducing
Contradicting	Contrasting	Extending
Debating	Deriving	Dismissing
Enthusing	Formulating	Demonstrating
Exemplifying	Modelling	Supporting
Amplifying	Qualifying	Extrapolating
Developing	Extemporizing	Proposing
Quantifying	Improvising	Hypothesizing

Not all of these ways of using words is likely to be relevant to a given topic in a given lecture in a particular discipline, of course. However, when used well, at appropriate points in a lecture, actions from the list above can cause far greater learning payoff than simply 'reading', 'reciting' or 'describing'.

But what about the students?

With the best will in the world, we can try to structure our lectures so that the words we choose to say (rather than put on screen or in handouts) are geared to cause students to think rather than transcribe, but it can all come to nothing unless students *know* what they should be trying to follow, and *why* we are choosing to get them thinking in the ways we have planned. This in itself is a strong rationale for sharing our route-map with students, rather than keeping it to ourselves as we lecture. Or at least we can start each lecture by setting the scene, for example by sharing the intended learning outcomes with the students. We can also finish the lecture by returning briefly to the intended learning outcomes, and identifying any that have yet to be addressed, perhaps in our next lecture, or perhaps by the students on their own or with each other, using sources and learning resources.

In this chapter we have concentrated on how what we do in our lectures needs to be inextricably bound up with what we want our students to be doing, there and then, as they sit in our lectures. We will return to this crucial agenda in the next-but-one chapter. Why next-but-one? We think it will be useful to go first into how best we can make use of some of the tools at our disposal in lecture theatres, to help our words to have even more effect, and indeed to extend the principles of using words well to our planning of appropriate sights and sounds to help students to learn in our lectures.

6 Lecturing tools

In former times, as our more senior colleagues sometimes remind us, the matter of 'tools in the lecture room' was quite straightforward. There were really only two: talk and chalk! Or, to be more accurate, chalk and blackboards. Every classroom had a blackboard. In many cases, every lecture theatre had one or more bigger blackboard – usually of the 'roller' variety, just about enough for a lecturer to write upon it for a whole hour without needing to rub anything out. Nowadays in the developed world, blackboards are becoming a something of a rarity, but they still have their champions. For example, the *Times Higher Education Supplement* in January 2002 reported hot debate at high-level strategy meetings at Oxford University about the replacement of blackboards by whiteboards in the lecture rooms of the associated Natural History Museum. Apparently the mathematicians who teach there argued that 'chalk has just the right edge on it to allow them to write at the correct speed to explain to students. Marker pens that glide across are considered too fast' (*THES*, Diary, 18 January 2002, p13).

So blackboards will remain part of the lecturer's toolkit for the time being at least, and as Donald Bligh reminds us in Chapter 10 of the latest edition of his seminal text, *What's the Use of Lectures?* (Bligh, 2000a), it is easy to forget that not all lecturing contexts worldwide are blessed with continuous and reliable supplies of electrical power with which to run the technological aids to presentation that can be really helpful in lectures. You may think not much can go wrong with these simple tools. They still work if there is a power-cut. Blackboards don't have bulbs that can blow. It is relatively straightforward to do sufficient forward planning to prevent the supply of chalk from running out – by maintaining stocks of it in the lecturer's dusty drawers, pockets, or handbag.

There are still things that can go wrong, however. Many blackboard users write illegibly and few have been given the kind of helpful advice that Bligh offers on chalkboard technique (Bligh, 2000a). Writing on boards can be tiring, chalk makes your clothes dusty and students commonly report that lecturers find it difficult to gauge what size writing can be seen from the rear seats of the lecture theatre. Chalk rubs off easily, smudges, and whatever is written is lost each time the board is cleaned. On the occasions when you try to get ahead of yourself by writing out the notes for a lecture in advance on a board, fate seems to decree that in the moments you are absent, someone decides to clean the board for you!

Roller blackboards are a great improvement over static boards but they can get shiny, marked with old chalk and the mechanism often gets stuck or the board itself torn. While roller boards have the advantage of allowing the lecturer to roll up the written script high to assist visibility, this often means that the bits that can be seen were being spoken about several moments ago, and students may find following the argument and writing down notes impossible to do in practice. For the lecturer of constrained height, there can be humiliating moments trying to reach up to grip the metal strip on the board that allows it to be rolled up or down.

Writing with marker pens on whiteboards can be an improvement, in that students can more readily see coloured pens on whiteboards than chalk on boards (Seymour and Snowberg, quoted in Bligh, 2000a). There are disadvantages however, to a method where the lecturer is working hard to write, speak and put ideas across at the same time (although many maths and science lecturers will argue that there is no better way to work through a proof or demonstrate how a complex set of ideas is built together than by doing it live on a board).

Inevitably, when using a whiteboard or a blackboard, lecturers tend to talk to the board rather than the students. It is certainly difficult to project your voice when writing with your back to the audience, and even when a microphone is used, opportunities to communicate direct with students through non-verbal cues and to keep an eye on what students are doing are hampered by facing away from rather than towards them.

Also, what students are doing can be dictated by what the lecturer is doing. Writing on boards tends to mean that students feel that they have to copy down absolutely everything that the lecturer writes. This is also true to some extent with any means of presentation in lectures, but when students see lecturers painstakingly writing material on the board, this provides indications that the lecturer feels these particular words are important and worthy of note. This is not necessarily a problem if what is written on the board is headlines or highlights, but when detailed material is written up to be copied down, students don't tend to have time to *think* about what it means, being so busy getting it all down into their notes.

Nowadays, the range of tools at the lecturer's disposal is much expanded for many of us. The most prestigious lecture rooms are equipped to the highest standards and technology abounds, which makes the whole process of delivery much more risky – if the technology fails, the lecturer becomes helpless. Students understandably can be very intolerant if they are kept waiting while the lecturer appears to be bungling around at the front, trying to remember the password needed to get a presentation to work on the lecture room PC. All too often the call goes out for a technician to come and sort out the mess, while precious minutes are lost. Students may not necessarily notice or comment on the structure, coherence and delivery of a lecture, but they certainly *will* be vocal when we don't use the tools of the lecturing trade well. As before, we offer a few hopefully representative voices to set the scene for what follows.

students' views ...

Dr Arbuthnott gives really polished lectures. I'm sure we all gave them top grades for presentation on the evaluation form at the end. We waited with bated breath to see if anything would go wrong – but it never did. There was plenty of impact – it made us think. Some of the things we saw were really memorable – I'll never forget those hilarious video clips! But I can't quite remember what the point that was being made at the time was, so it was all a bit of a waste really.

The next time some idiot thinks that they can just photocopy a page from a book onto an overhead, or scan it in and then expect us to be able to read it in class, I'm going to scream! Why doesn't she step back to any seat beyond row three and see that it's impossible to see that level of detail without a telescope? And she always says, 'Oh dear, this one doesn't seem to be very clear.' Why doesn't she look for herself? When she asks if we can see it ok, we all tell her we can't but she carries on regardless!

If I knew how to, I would disconnect the link from the PC in the lecture room to the Internet. Every time the lecturer wants to show us something live on the Internet, it takes ages to log on and then the connection always fails. We seem to waste hours of time and then the rest of the lecture content is rushed or cut. When I wanted to do something similar when I did my seminar presentation to other students, rather than taking a risk I copied screen dumps into my presentation and showed what you would see if you logged on. Some of this lot seem to be so pleased with themselves because they have found some relevant sites that they don't think through the logistics of the actual lecture.

My problem was the exam. I'd revised the notes as well as anything else I revised, but when I saw the questions, it was as though the wrong question paper had been put on my exam desk. It had the right subject details on it, though. I think what had happened was that we'd got so caught up in watching the clever effects that were used in the presentations that we'd not really got down to working out what it actually *meant* in the context of the subject of the lectures. I'm more careful now – I try to make sure that I'm not just enjoying what's going on in lectures, but trying to work out how it all links together to the sort of questions that we may be given when it comes to the exam at the end of the course.

Lecturers often have mixed feelings about new technologies too.

the lecturers ...

Dr Arbuthnott

I *like* the technology of the large-group lecture. It's a bit like when I was a kid getting all of my train set working. Everything has to be in its place. It has to run like clockwork. When I go to conferences, I am amazed at how sloppy many of the presenters are with their presentations. There's no point showing a PowerPoint slide (or an overhead, or a projection slide, or a Web download, or a live Web link) if the people at the back can't read anything that is on the screen. And each PowerPoint presentation has to be just right – all slides in the same format, for coherence you know. None of this fiddling about with different coloured backgrounds for me – that just gets in the way. And students need to have a copy of everything they're going to see in my lectures in their hands at the start of the lecture – no point them just copying it all down. If they want to see the finer points again (like how I put together the pieces of the jigsaw by animating my slides) they can see it again and again on their computers by downloading the slides from the intranet.

It's about being professional, I suppose – I spend ages on getting the technology right for each new lecture, and then polish it immediately after that lecture so that it's even better next time. I've had nothing but praise from my peer-reviewers about my usage of the technologies in the lecture theatre. Even the external examiner came in to see how I showed students how to get their heads round that tricky concept in Module 4. I suppose I've now got a bit of a reputation; the staff development people get me to give a demo lecturette to the Academic Practice Certificate lot in Semester 2. They usually clap at the end.

Marisa

It's like the flight deck of Concorde in the new lecture room. I haven't had my briefing from the technician yet, so I'm scared to touch the control panel, other than to use the (clearly marked) switch to raise and dim the main lights. It reminds me a bit of the cinemas of my childhood, with screens going up and down. I half expect to see the Hammond organ emerge from the pit at the front!

Louise

Rushing in at the last minute from the hospital, it's always nerve-wracking hoping that my disk will work with the PC, finding it won't and then getting one of the students to help me. Mostly I just stick to the overhead projector we insisted they leave in there in front of the demonstration bench. I prefer my own monochrome transparencies anyway, and you can get lots more on a slide that way.

So what tools have we to master now?

The range of tools available in well-equipped lecture theatres in affluent countries now rarely includes chalk or blackboards but may include any number of the following:

- One or more overhead projectors, and sloping screens mounted high up, so there's no 'keystoning' effect (see below).
- A data projector, either suspended from the ceiling, or beaming through from the projection box at the back of the theatre, and a huge screen visible from everywhere in the theatre, and bearing the words in red on a label at the bottom: 'Do not write on this projection screen' (but someone usually has).
- A whiteboard at one side, with the right kind of marker pens already there, which don't squeak like chalk.
- A computer on the demonstration bench at the front of the theatre, and a lead where laptops can be connected directly to the data projector.

- The computer may be connected via a modem to the intranet or the Internet at will, so that live links and searches can be done in front of the whole group.
- A radio mouse, so the lecturer can be anywhere in the theatre and still move the on-screen cursor to the bit that's being talked about on the current slide, or move on to the next one, and so on.
- A radio mike, so that the lecturer can mingle with the students and still talk to everyone, and even get particular students to be heard by the whole throng.
- A fixed mike at the rostrum at the front, for those lecturers who like presenting from a lectern.
- An epidiascope which can beam up on the big screen not only overhead transparencies, but at the flick of a switch, a handout, or better still a column or two from today's paper, or this week's new journal issue – and with a zoom control so that a particular paragraph can be big enough on-screen to be read with ease by everyone.
- A touch-sensitive screen, which (if you've not forgotten your glasses) you can use to dim the lights, close the window blinds, switch the projector from laptop to video, and even silence the air-conditioning for a couple of minutes while the students listen carefully to the sound-track of that carefully chosen interview clip.
- A 'help' button or phone to use in an emergency to alert the chief technician that there's a problem with any of the equipment.

There's one important tool *missing* in most lecture theatres we've worked in: a waste bin. The consequence of this omission is that the front area still has a fascinating collection of other people's left-over handout fragments, at least three kinds of evaluation pro-forma, and the odd overhead transparency that has been left by someone who may well be about to notice its absence, live, in a lecture theatre elsewhere on the campus. If one uses overhead transparencies, a system to file and keep them in the right order is invaluable (rather than just bundling them up together randomly) as both authors will testify! Many people also find it useful to have on hand a small screwdriver for tightening the old overhead projector head, which gradually succumbs to the effects of gravity without the lecturer noticing, but with *all* the students noticing, or for disengaging one's laptop from the projection system.

From the student perspective, some of the better theatres can be really comfortable learning environments – soft seats, plenty of legroom, pleasant balanced humidity and temperature, and soft lighting to see the on-screen images clearly. Very close, in fact, to the natural conditions for inducing human sleep, especially in early-morning and evening lectures, when students who may have been doing shift work late into the previous night need to sleep.

In this chapter, we'll concentrate on some of the technology-based tools that we can put to use when working with large classes in lecture environments. One of the most versatile tools is the handout, but we look at that in more detail in Chapter 7 on what you can get students to do in lectures, since they can't cause learning to happen by themselves.

Fit-for-purpose usage of lecture-room tools

Like tools in any other context, the technologies that are now at our disposal in our lecture theatres can be used well, or can be used badly. When the technologies at our disposal are used *really well* to help students to understand concepts, the students don't notice the tools as such: they capture the intended learning points addressed by our use of the tools.

When our usage of the tools is spectacular, the impact at the time may be high, but the learning payoff is likely to be less. The technology can get in the way of the intended learning. When we use the tools badly, students are unlikely to regard what they are seeing to be important because they are distracted by what they see as incompetence.

Marshall McLuhan's perhaps over-used aphorism suggests that 'the medium is the message'. So if the medium is used badly, students subconsciously will think the message is unimportant. If the medium is used well, they will find the message more credible. But the medium should not get in the way of the message – in other words it should not be used *too* well for comfort. Striking the right balance is no mean feat.

Many (including ourselves) have published advice, tips and suggestions on how to make the most of the tools of the trade that can be used in lectures (Bligh, 2002; Brown and Race, 1995; Gibbs and Jenkins, 1992; Hogan, J in Fry *et al*, 1999; Race, 1999a). Here we provide guidance on selected aspects and particularly concentrate on the desired *effects* of using the various technologies to help students to get more out of lectures, and the *consequences* of getting it wrong!

From blackboards to whiteboards?

Most lecture theatres still have surfaces for us to write upon, with chalk or marker pens. There are also some subjects where blackboards remain favoured lecture-room tools, for example maths, science and engineering lecturers often tell us of the advantages of students being able to *watch* them write out derivations and proofs before their eyes, and hearing their lecturers explaining what they are doing as they write. One *could* write the same things onto overhead transparency film, but it's easy to be dazzled by the glare while doing so, and it's not quite the same as using a blackboard or whiteboard. However, many readers of this book will remember attending lectures where two side-by-side roller blackboards would be filled over an hour, while they tried to copy down everything that the lecturer wrote on them.

Whiteboards can be used for many of the purposes served by blackboards, and without the hazard of chalk dust. However, chalk was relatively straightforward to remove from blackboards. Marker pens come in many varieties. 'Dry-wipe' pens are the best for writing on whiteboards, as writing can be erased with a soft cloth or tissue. Other types of water-based pen can be used where a damp or wet cloth is all that is needed to remove what we've written, but 'permanent' markers, usually solvent-based, which are fine for flipcharts, can be real trouble with whiteboards! Even using a good solvent, it is often impossible to remove the last traces of writing left on whiteboards after the wrong sort of pen has been used. Many is the unfortunate lecturer who has resorted to using (only sometimes successfully) aftershave, perfume, or whisky to prevent the evidence of having used the wrong sort of pen on whiteboards being seen by all! If you do use the wrong kind of pen on a whiteboard and it's recent, you can write over the text with the right kinds of pen and it will act as a solvent. If it's old, nothing short of the appropriate commercially produced cleaner will shift it and substitutes you may wish to try out normally damage the board further.

In some of the literature on teaching and lecturing, particularly the sources mentioned at the start of this chapter, there is detailed and sensible advice on how to use chalkboards and marker boards well. Suggestions include:

- Remember not to talk to the board while writing on it – the class may not be able to hear!
- Be aware that visually impaired students will be at a loose end while you are writing, so let them know what you are doing and reassure them about how they will be able to access your notes.
- Don't forget to look round now and then to see what the students are doing while you're writing something up for them – they may have gone away, mentally or physically!

- Make sure that your writing is big enough to be seen at the back of the room.
- Remember that for at least some of the time, you will be physically between the writing you're doing and some of the students – don't erase it till they've all had time to see it.
- The sound of squeaking chalk can set students' teeth on edge, distracting them from what you want them to be thinking about.
- Be aware that whatever you might write up on a board during a lecture may be very similar to what you'll have to do all over again next time you give a similar lecture.

Despite some of what we've said, blackboards and whiteboards have one very significant advantage in lectures: whatever's written on them can be there for students to see for quite some time. It doesn't disappear at the click of a mouse or the push of a remote-control button. There are some things that are well worth being visible for a substantial part of most lectures, not least the intended learning outcomes that will be the focus of the lecture, or the list of six main factors being analysed and explored during the lecture.

The rest of this chapter focuses on the relative newcomer to lecture environments: the big (white) screen. The first thing *not* to do with this screen is write on it with a marker pen – or coloured chalk (see above). It's best not to touch this screen at all. This is where several other tools come in – the ways and means of putting images up on this screen – to help to turn your lecture into an audio-visual experience rather than simply an auditory one. There's a lot of evidence that most people learn more from things that they both see and hear (and much more evidence suggesting that people learn even more from what they *do* with what they see and hear). So how best can we use the big screen to get our students really learning things during our lectures?

Using on-screen words and images

Visibility and illumination

Whether what's on-screen in the lecture theatre is coming from an overhead projector, a data projector, a video projector, or a still-slides projector, there are some key attributes that should be achieved on screen. For a start, words, numbers and other features should be *readable*. That particularly means readable by the students towards the back of the theatre. But it also means that *all parts of what's on the screen* should be readable by everyone. That in turn often means we should only be using the top half (or at most two-thirds) of the screen for anything that's really important, unless the screen is large and placed high in the lecture theatre. How often do we notice, when our final bullet point on a slide appears at the bottom of the screen, that many students have to move their heads so that they can see it? They need to see over or round the students sitting in front of them.

Visibility of what's on screen naturally depends on the level of background illumination in the lecture room. In purpose-built lecture theatres, there is often no daylight to worry about, and lighting that can be controlled. There are spotlights to light us up when we really want students to be watching us explain things. The lights at the front of the theatre can be dimmed to make the images on screen visible, while leaving sufficient lighting from the back of the theatre so that students can still see well enough to make notes. However, probably the majority of lectures are given in classrooms where lighting is not so optimal. Problems we have met (frequently!) include:

- rooms where there is only one light switch – the lights are either full on, or off;
- lighting that shines directly onto the screen: overhead projector images can be used, but data projected images are not bright enough to be seen properly;
- classrooms where the sun may shine directly onto the screen at a certain time of the day, and where reflections from other buildings hit the same screen at other times of the day (checking the room out at 8.30 in the morning may suggest there will be no problems with lighting, but going in at 2 in the afternoon gives an unpleasant surprise);
- rooms where although there are blinds or curtains, they have become damaged or no longer work, and there is no way of stopping daylight from being a problem;
- problems for students with visual impairments/dyslexia caused by lighting conditions (see Chapter 10 on inclusive lecturing).

When using presentation managers such as PowerPoint in such classrooms, it can be a real problem for students with or without visual impairments if the presentation format uses dark backgrounds and white or yellow print. It is best then to have light backgrounds and dark print. In a well-designed lecture theatre, it often looks much more attractive to use the former. In practice, when the same presentation may sometimes be used in a good lecture theatre, and at other times in a relatively light classroom, it can be worth the few minutes it can take to have two different presentations to choose from, by making alternative versions for use in light and dark rooms. This is relatively easily done by choosing different options on the master slide for the respective conditions, and saving the files separately on disk. However, changing the master slide does not always change things that may have been imported into the presentation (for example slides copied from a different presentation), so it's necessary to check through each presentation and attend manually to those slides that need adjustment.

'Keystoning'

Ceiling-mounted data projectors (or equipment located in a projection box at the back of larger theatres) usually project head-on to the screen, and give a rectangular image. Keystoning is the effect you get when using overhead projectors, slide projectors or data projectors when the image hits the screen at an angle or from below, rather than head-on. Normally, the tendency is for the bottom of the image to be narrower on-screen than the top of the image. Countless lecturers have worked perfectly well around this, since so long as the image is readable, there's not really a problem for students.

Many lecture theatres now have highly mounted sloping projection screens, so that an overhead projector can beam up at them without keystoning occurring. Some theatres have two such screens, one at each side of a central large vertical screen, so that projection from a data projector or projection box can use the central screen, and from one or two overhead projectors on the smaller sloping screens. However, there are still many teaching rooms for large classes where the situation is more basic. Sometimes where there is just one screen, it may be fixed vertically (or of course just be a blank wall). Alternatively, the screen may be adjustable to a slight angle away from vertical, to reduce or eliminate keystoning when using an overhead projector.

One of the advantages of overhead projectors is that you can swivel the image up and down by simply moving the mirror that usually reflects the image towards the screen. When using data or slide projectors, this is less likely to be an option. Some such instruments have swivelling mirrors too, but most beam straight from the machine, which means that the only way of altering the angle at which the light beams out is to put the machine itself on a slope – a dangerous thing to do with expensive (and sometimes heavy) equipment.

Keystoning, when it occurs with a well-prepared slide presentation, often seems more annoying than with an overhead projector – for example a bullet point at the top of the screen will be larger than one at the bottom of the screen, and for students sitting at a distance it can appear that things at the top of the screen are somehow more important than the rest (and indeed more readable than the rest). Keystoning is perhaps most irritating when projecting images of diagrams, flowcharts or photographs, when the distortion produced can be confusing and detract from the intended realism. However, modern data projectors have a keystoning adjustment feature, which can usually be found by pressing a 'menu' button on the machine. This allows you to adjust the on-screen image until it is rectangular again, even when hitting the screen at an angle.

Using overhead projectors

The overhead projector has been for some time a fairly standard piece of equipment in most rooms used for teaching large groups in countries in the developed world. There is usually one (or more) in any large lecture theatre, sometimes sitting on the lecture bench, and often installed permanently there, positioned appropriately to project onto a fixed or adjustable screen. Despite the fact that overhead projectors are relatively simple instruments, a wide variety of models exist. The position of the on/off and focusing controls can be quite different from one machine to another. There is nothing more embarrassing than to walk up to an overhead projector, with hundreds of students watching you, and not know how to switch that particular one on! It's well worth checking out in advance how to work the machine in each teaching room you encounter. Nip in between lectures, or first thing in the morning, and play with the machine you're going to use until you have no such worries. It's particularly worth getting to known the 'fringe control' adjustments on most machines. You use these to adjust the image so that it's as sharp as it can be right across the screen, and to avoid coloured fringes appearing at the edges of the image. A good way of getting this exactly right is to prepare one transparency photocopied from some very small print – not to use with students, of course, but so that you can fine-tune the adjustment of the projector with it.

Most overhead projectors come with two bulbs – the one you're using, and the one that blew last week but no one said anything about! It is, however, worth checking out how to switch between one and the other, so that when the bulb blows while you're using it, you've got the chance of switching to the other one, if it's there. It can be highly embarrassing to summon technical help, only for the technician to come in and flick a switch to put you back in business. And if you *are* the person for whom the bulb blows, make sure to tell someone about it so that your successor in the room doesn't inherit the problem.

Overhead projectors come with different sized platens – the glass sheet on which you lay your transparencies. Most are roughly square, and usually just a little less in dimension than the length of an A4 sheet of paper. This can be a problem if you are printing off overheads from desktop publishing software or word-processing formats on A4 sheets, or (more commonly) producing your transparencies from a photocopier. It's not a problem when using 'portrait' orientation – you can easily slip the overhead up the screen if you need to show something that is right at the bottom of your transparency. But if you're using the transparencies 'landscape', and the transparency fills the whole width of the sheet, you may find that it is just impossible to project the whole image. It's irritating to have to keep juggling it from left to right so that students can see the whole of the flowchart at once, for example. It is therefore wise to make sure that none of your transparencies will use the whole of an A4 sheet's width when used 'landscape'. That said, it is normally better to use 'landscape' than 'portrait' in most lecture rooms, because of the need to avoid putting anything too low down on the screen, causing the visibility problems we mentioned earlier.

There is another situation you may encounter. Some overhead projectors are built with a platen that is exactly A4. This is fine, provided that it is A4 the way you want to use it – but if some of your transparencies are 'portrait' and others are 'landscape', it can be a nuisance. These machines usually allow you to change from one to the other, by rotating the projector head (containing the mirror) and sometimes rotating the machine itself through 90 degrees (which is fine if the machine is free standing, but not an option if it is fixed). Therefore, it's also worth checking out in advance how you're going to do this, if you need to in your lectures.

All this talk about making sure that you know how to make the machine work for you can be to no avail, of course, if once you're using it you don't use it well. There are many tips and wrinkles for checking that your transparencies do you justice in your lectures. The following list is adapted from Race (2000):

- *Make good-looking slides.* Good-quality overheads can add credibility to your messages. It's worth using desktop publishing programs to make your principal overhead transparencies look professional and believable. With inkjet and laser colour printers, it's nowadays relatively easy to produce coloured transparencies with graphics.

- *Be careful with coloured print or writing.* As we've said elsewhere, some colours, especially red, are harder than you might imagine to see from the back of a large room. Throw away any orange or yellow overhead pens – unless you're using them for colouring in blocks on diagrams or flowcharts for example.

- *Don't use typewritten overheads.* To be clearly visible, most fonts need to be at sizes 18, 24, or larger – considerably bigger and bolder than typical typewritten materials. Make sure that each transparency you prepare will be visible from the back of the largest room you are likely to use, even by someone without good eyesight.

- *Keep the number of words down.* A good overhead transparency only needs to contain the main ideas, not the details. You can add the details as you discuss the main points on the transparencies.

- *Watch students' eyes.* As soon as you notice students having to move their head positions to see something on one of your transparencies, it's worth trying to move that part up so that they can see it without moving their gaze. Use the top half of the screen. By sliding your transparencies up, you can normally make the most important pieces of information appear towards the top of the screen and thus more easily visible by students at your sessions.

- *Get your transparencies into the right order before your lecture.* There's nothing worse than watching a lecturer sifting and sorting to try and find the right overhead. It's sometimes worth arranging them into two sets: ones you will *definitely* use, and ones you *might* wish to use if time permits, or if anticipated questions arise.

- *Try not to read out your overheads word for word!* Your students can usually read much faster than you can speak. People don't like having things read out to them that they can read for themselves. However, keep in mind the comments made about special needs in Chapter 10.

- *Minimize passive transcribing by students.* Copying down words from transparencies is not the most productive of learning activities. Where possible, issue handout materials that already contain the wording from your principal overhead transparencies.

- *Don't point at the screen itself.* This would mean losing eye contact with your students. Use a pen or pencil to rest on the transparency, indicating the part you're talking about.

- *Be prepared to add things to your transparencies during discussions.* This ability to edit slides 'live' is an advantage overhead projectors have over computer-based presentation managers (unless you are a very skilled and confident PowerPoint user), and can help your students to feel that their comments are important and valued. With transparencies produced from inkjet printers, however, don't write on your original (you can often damage the ink on the original slide); instead put a blank sheet of acetate over it!
- *Don't over-use 'progressive reveal' techniques* (showing transparencies a bit at a time by gradually moving a masking sheet of paper). Some students feel manipulated if they are continually 'controlled' in this way. You also look a nerd when the paper you are using to conceal the bottom bit of the slide keeps falling off! It can be better to build up a complex overhead using multiple overlays.
- *Remember to switch the projector off!* Most overhead projectors make at least some noise. When you're not actually showing something, it's important that both visually and aurally you are not distracting your students.

Sometimes, in main lecture theatres, you'll have the chance to use overhead projection facilities that are much more sophisticated than the straightforward machines discussed so far. For example, you may come across machines which transmit images of your transparencies through a central projection system and beam them onto the screen for you, but with additional controls such as zoom and focus on a touch-screen control panel, and an image of exactly what's on-screen on a monitor, so you can see what your students can see without turning round to look behind you. These machines usually allow you to project from paper as well, such as handouts, an open textbook, a newspaper page, a photograph and so on, by flicking a switch which turns the machine into epidiascope mode.

This can be really useful if you choose to show a relevant extract from today's paper, to add currency to your lecture, and zoom in to a particular paragraph so that even students at the back of the theatre can read the print clearly. It goes without saying that these more complex systems take a bit of mastering to use them at their best. On average, we suggest, you find an hour or so where you can play with the equipment in the empty theatre, and gain confidence and familiarity with it. Better still, if possible have someone with expertise like the technician assigned to that room to give you a guided tour of what it can do, then practise when they've gone.

Data projectors, computers and laptops

Most principal lecture rooms in the developed world are quite high-tech environments. The demonstration bench at the front is often equipped with a computer, keyboard, mouse and a bewildering array of controls. It can feel like encountering a flight control console! Sometimes there is a touch-screen control panel with which you can:

- dim the theatre lighting to various preset positions, or on a sliding scale right down to darkness;
- open and shut blinds or curtains to control daylight getting in to the theatre;
- move a main projection screen up or down;
- adjust the microphone volume;
- get the lights back on (it's really useful to be confident about how to do this!);
- switch on the ceiling-mounted data projector;
- switch the projected display from laptop to computer and back again, so that you can show (for example) live Web links on the big screen, and then switch seamlessly to your PowerPoint slide containing a list of questions to get students to think about what they've just seen;
- choose between options such as CD ROM, DVD, videotape and so on from what's in the computer equipment;
- adjust the sound volume when using audio-visual aids;
- turn on a pre-loaded slide projector, for those things where the on-screen image needs to be more precise than can be achieved with digital display systems or where you are using slides of images from an established slide library;
- switch various spotlights on and off so that students can, for example, still see your face while you explain to them what's on-screen; and so on.

But while lecturers like our character Dr Arbuthnott may revel in such sophistication, it can be somewhat intimidating to most of us, especially if we only give the occasional lecture in the theatre concerned.

More often, it's a case of availability of 'some of the above'. Many more-conventional teaching rooms now have ceiling mounted data projectors, and a computer and keyboard (usually in a locked cupboard near the front). There's usually also a data cable ready to plug into the appropriate socket on a laptop computer, which means you can work direct from your own machine rather than having to transfer presentations to floppy disk or CD and insert it into the equipment which lives in the room. As before, there's no substitute for a dry run. Setting up your laptop, or slipping your disk into the existing machine goes much more smoothly when there aren't lots of eyes watching your every move.

Even more often, it seems, it's a case of 'almost none of the above'. Lecturers who become comfortable with (for example) PowerPoint presentations often find that there are so many advantages of using it that it's worth taking all the steps necessary to bring it right there to the students, even in relatively plain large teaching rooms. There may well be a suitable screen or blank wall in the room, but it's then up to you to bring in and set up a data projector, and connect it to your laptop yourself. Many institutions have 'bookable' data projectors, and a technician will bring in the machine and help you to set it up shortly before your lecture (if, of course, you've booked it in time, and if, of course, there are plenty of machines to go round, and if...!) Or you might even be lucky enough to have your own data projector. In any of these cases, you've got the additional matter of having to find a good place to put the projector itself. It may need to be a few rows back, to get the image big enough for students to see. You're almost certain, one time or another, to need a power extension lead, to get the power to the machine and to your laptop. You'll also almost certainly need to equip yourself with an appropriate data lead to connect the two – one a few metres longer than the short one that came with the projector originally! You need to be able to get yourself far enough away from the projector itself so that you don't get in the way of the projected image as you fiddle with your laptop. This brings the danger of a lot of tangled leads – and that is not just a nuisance but also a safety hazard. Conference venues, you may have noticed, go to the trouble of sticking cables down to the floor with wide black tape, to comply with safety regulations.

Well-practised technophiles like our character Dr Arbuthnott seem able to come into a plain room and transform it ready for PowerPoint and Web connections in just a few minutes. For the rest of us, there's a learning curve to ascend, including mastering some simple points such as those below:

- Often, there's an order in which you must connect things together and switch them on. For example, it's usually necessary to connect up your data projector to your laptop, and switch the projector on before you power-up your laptop. Otherwise, the laptop doesn't 'know' that there's a data projector there, or what sort of data projector it is. Sometimes, your laptop will give you a menu about finding the best 'driver' for the 'new hardware' that it's detected. You'll have several mouse-clicks to make before the image appears on the screen – anxious moments, even for hardened technophiles.

- Remote controls can be really useful – or cause nightmares. There may be one remote control that controls just the functions of the data projector, such as focus, brilliance and so on, and another that 'speaks' to your laptop and can help you go from one slide to another. In the case of the laptop, it needs to recognize that there's one there, otherwise it may be only your trackpad or mouse that controls it.

- It's good to be able to turn the 'display' off. Some projectors allow you to get a blank black screen by pressing a button on the machine or on the remote control, but on some the whole machine goes into standby mode, and perhaps closes down. It then takes minutes to get it all going again when you want to resume your PowerPoint show – and *these* minutes, with all the students waiting, pass much more slowly than the same minutes when you were setting up in an empty room! However, when using PowerPoint, if you press the 'B' key on most keyboards, you go straight to a black screen without doing anything to the projector. When you want to resume your display, pressing 'B' again brings it back. Furthermore, pressing 'P' on the keyboard can take you straight to the previous slide, or 'N' to the next one. Sometimes remote controls have forward and backward gears, but more often it's a mouse-click to go forward and no way of getting back, which is where it's really handy to have a 'P'.

Using presentation packages

The most commonly available of these currently is Microsoft PowerPoint and advice on how to design and use PowerPoint presentations is widely available through commercial training packages (including online materials), through institutional training programmes and elsewhere. The advice offered in Bligh (2000a) is also detailed and helpful.

Use of colour

Now that we *can*, it is very tempting to use every colour in the rainbow! However, many lecturers have found that not all colours are equally visible from the back of a large room (and indeed there are issues for students with dyslexia and those who cannot readily discriminate colours from one another). Even for those with normal colour vision, yellow and orange are often problematic, and text or numbers in red are very difficult for many people to discern at a distance, although they might be perfectly ok at near or middle distances. The same text in the same size in black or another dark colour may cause no such problems when viewed from a distance.

If using PowerPoint or similar packages, there are a number of ready-prepared layouts for use that are easy to customize, but if you are printing onto overheads, remember that colour printing is expensive and can be time-consuming, so should not be undertaken lightly. Students may be very familiar with most of the most common designs, which might be a novelty to new users but for the students may be a bore.

Fonts

Most on-screen words these days are word-processed – whether for PowerPoint slides, Web sites, or well-produced overhead transparencies. Word processing packages arm us with a plethora of different fonts (typefaces), and it becomes very tempting to make full use of the range at our disposal – but at our peril! For a start, it can be very irritating for readers to see several different fonts on a single slide. While this may be satisfactory for those occasions where we want to emphasize a particular word here and there by putting it into a different font, it is now accepted that it is best to keep the changes to a minimum. Additionally, over-elaborate fonts can provide difficulties for students with visual impairments or dyslexia. With PowerPoint slides, it can be useful to have one particular font (and colour) for the title, and then to continue (for example with sub-topics or bullet points) in a different font or colour.

Live links

These should be used with caution, as delays and unusable links can be annoying for our audiences. With PowerPoint, you can insert hot-links to all sorts of things using the 'Action Buttons' facility. These links can be clicked using the mouse or remote control while on-screen in the lecture theatre and, if a suitable modem connection is up and running, take you straight to the Web site, or photo, or different PowerPoint presentation, and so on. It is, of course, important to make sure that you can get *back* to your presentation when you want to. It is sometimes more difficult than you think, as you might need to click an 'X' box at the top right-hand corner of the screen to do so, and this might not be possible with the particular remote control you're using, or might be quite hard to do with nervous fingers using your mouse or the trackpad on your laptop.

When we link on-screen into Web pages, the problem of visibility and readability can become serious. From the back of the room, it may only be the main headings that can be seen well at all. This is not to say that you should never show Web pages on-screen in lectures; you may simply want students to register the general appearance of some pages so that they are primed to recognize them more readily when they subsequently search them out for themselves. Or we may just want students in the lecture to see a particular graphic, chart, diagram, table or photo, rather than the small-print wording surrounding it. All this is fine so long as we make our intentions clear at the time. In other words, if we say, 'Just look at this' and point to it with our on-screen cursor or laser pointer and add, 'Don't try to read the text here, wait till you've got the Web page on your own machine', then no one is likely to become frustrated by what they *can't* read there in the lecture room. However, the students sitting at the front are still going to be advantaged – or even distracted – by actually being able to see both the words and the image we're referring to.

Using 'Action Buttons' to give ourselves room for manoeuvre

Suppose you've got a fairly long PowerPoint presentation for a lecture (or perhaps even for a half-day short course). Suppose there are 63 slides in all. Human nature being what it is, the chances of wanting to show *all* 63 slides are low. If we'd had it on overhead transparencies, we'd probably have missed some out on occasion. Moreover, the chances of us wanting to show the 63 slides *in one particular order* are rather remote. If we'd had it on overheads, we'd probably have pulled one out of the 'shown' pile now and again to return to a point raised by a student asking a question, for example. In other words, we can end up feeling somewhat frustrated that we can't get back and forwards through the 63 slides at will. We can, of course, go backwards and forwards manually, or even use the 'slide navigation' command, but that's rather clumsy. Furthermore, what about all those 'optional extra' slides or short sequences we might like to have available to us, ready to use if we see that a particular point we're making in the lecture needs a bit more explanation or elaboration?

It's all possible. Especially when working from your own laptop, you can have a 'menu' slide linking to anything and everything of your choice on it. However, for most lectures, a menu that gets you to each of the main things you're likely to need would be sufficient and could look similar to the one shown in Figure 6.1.

Such a 'menu' slide can be placed *behind* each slide in a presentation, by pasting it into the Master Slide for the presentation as an Action Button, for example at the bottom right-hand corner of the slide, as shown in Figure 6.2.

You could leave the Action Button so that it would be visible in each of the slides in the presentation, but it is less distracting to make it invisible, by selecting the button, then choosing 'no fill' on the fill menu, and 'no line' on the lines menu. Then, on any slide, moving the on-screen cursor to the bottom right-hand corner and clicking takes you straight to the 'menu' slide, and clicking any of the action

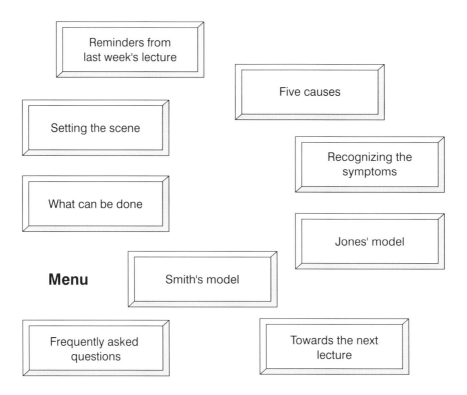

Figure 6.1 A menu slide

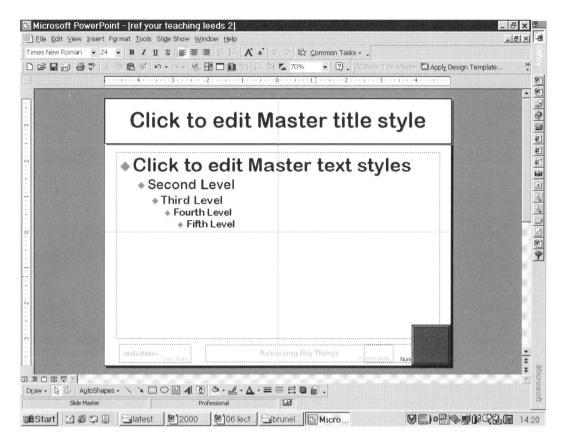

Figure 6.2 The menu slide as an Action Button

buttons then takes you to the other things you might want to show. To get back to your original presentation all you have to do is press the 'escape' key on the keyboard (but you can't get back directly just with a remote control). Alternatively, if it's only a single slide you've gone to through your menu, as soon as you click the mouse or remote control once more, you go straight back to your original presentation. The same happens automatically if your menu choice is another PowerPoint presentation, as soon as you reach the end of that one.

In a lecture course, for example, your 'menu' slide could link back and forward to all the other important slides that you use, so that you could quite quickly and spontaneously remind students of something they saw weeks ago, when a question comes up that makes this useful. Or you could end a lecture by skipping forward to the first couple of slides you'll use at the next lecture, for example to alert them to the intended learning outcomes that will be the next part of their agenda.

You can of course take it further, and have different hidden links behind various positions on each slide of your main presentation, but it becomes too easy to forget which one you located where! The 'menu' solution usually proves easiest in practice. One problem that arises is when you may need to transfer your main presentation to a floppy disk to put in a computer already in the lecture venue, in which case you need also to include any of the other presentations or links that you're intending to use during that lecture, along with your 'menu' slide itself.

'Now you see it, now it's gone'

This is perhaps the most significant problem of using sophisticated technology in lectures. When we're using a lot of different on-screen images, how much of it all do students remember an hour or two (let alone a week or two) after our lecture? It's easy enough to give students printouts of our PowerPoint slides, for example using the software's handout options of printing three-per-page with room for them to write notes alongside, or six-per-page if all they need are the slides themselves. But if we're linking to other things such as Web pages, we can't realistically print all these out too – in any case, we may be doing a Web search and moving around, and this will be different every time. And, like any other handouts, they aren't really being learnt from unless we're getting students to *do* something with them.

We can, however, put the PowerPoint sequences, containing the links, onto an intranet, so that students can repeat the tour for themselves, and go on their own diversions. But the problem of 'now you see it, now it's gone' continues to apply at least to some extent. We know only too well that it's possible to sit at a computer for an hour, totally absorbed, but not really have a firm grip on what we've been learning from it, unless we do more than just browse through some software applications or tour the Internet or follow up links.

Don't panic

What about 'Now you see it, now it *is* gone'? Just about everyone we know has tales to tell of when the technology let them down, in front of large groups of students, unexpectedly and irretrievably. One or more of the following can happen at any time, any of which can take the technological side of your roadshow right off the road:

- a power cut – everything goes dark except the emergency exit lights;
- a fire in the building, which means you've got to evacuate Theatre 2, leaving your laptop with all your stuff in it until tomorrow morning when the fumes that came in through the air conditioning system have been deemed by the fire service to have gone;
- nothing happens when you press 'next slide' on the remote control;
- the bulb blows in the data projector up on the ceiling;
- the computer goes down;
- the computer won't 'talk' to the data projector although it did so yesterday;
- the image on the big screen is just the top left two-thirds of what's on your laptop screen;
- the Web site you're connecting to has gone down;
- alerts about your new e-mails keep coming up on the big screen when you're linked in to the system;
- you can't find the file on your computer, and your floppy disk backup has corrupted.

It's enough to put anyone off using anything more than chalk and talk. But it happens. The main thing is to panic only inwardly. Your students will be *really* attentive now, watching how you rise to the challenges that beset you. You really want to just sit there and cry, but that's not what you want them to remember.

'I'll just give it another try' can be famous last words. Sometimes, we *know* we know what to do, and that it will work. But we've all been there on those days where someone found, all too slowly, that there was nothing that could be done in the time available. It's the technological equivalent of completely forgetting one's lines on-stage, except that there's not usually a helpful prompt from the wings to put one back on track. It is true that on some occasions a helpful student will know what to do and will bale us out.

Our best advice for these emergency situations, is to choose one or more of the following tactics for handling the crisis:

- Smile to yourself (through your teeth if necessary), then smile at the students and get them smiling back at you.
- Think of something for the students to do for five minutes. It's really useful if you *always* have with you something for the students to do for five minutes. Have it on an overhead, so you can show it

if it's not the overhead projector that is out of action – then they can remind themselves of what they're doing while you have a go at sorting out the problem for a moment or two.

- Alternatively, get them discussing and arguing with each other about something you've already done in the lecture. Give them a decision to make, something that they'll have different views about.
- Whatever you get *them* to do, now's your time for planning what *you're* going to do next. If what you *were* going to do next remains dependent upon the technology, it's time to find something else that isn't.
- Remember that it's not going to be an eternity till the end of the session. The time remaining will pass much more quickly for your students if they're engaged in something interesting.
- Perhaps turn it into a question-and-answer session. Ask the students to cluster into small buzz groups, and for each group to think of a question they'd like the answer to (preferably about the topic you'd been addressing, but not necessarily), and to jot questions down on slips of paper and pass them down to you at the front. You can then choose some questions you already know the answers to first, and work towards those questions you may wish to throw back at the whole group.
- Accept that there is likely to be some adjusting you'll need to do to your next couple of sessions, to get back on track to covering what you'd hoped to do before things went wrong. The problem then is if something goes wrong in your *only* lecture with that group of students: there are always ways of re-scheduling the event if really necessary.

Most lecturers who seem to sail serenely like swans through technical disasters have learnt to do so by trial and error. It's always a useful learning experience for us when our plans are thwarted – indeed it can bring us back down to earth and get us thinking with the students again. But it's uncomfortable and unwelcome, and uses up far more of our energy than we'd like. Therefore, having at least *one* emergency tactic can be a comfort for us at any time, and a lifesaver now and then.

Conclusion

Much of this book is about the pedagogy of making lectures work. This chapter, however, could be described as being mostly about the 'technogogy'! In practice, we need to make the most of both to ensure that our lectures are useful learning experiences for our students. The most polished technical performances in the world don't compensate for any lack of pedagogical design in our lectures. Similarly, the most astute pedagogical creations can be rendered useless if we use the lecture-room technologies awkwardly, badly, or inappropriately, especially as it is this side of things which students experience immediately.

It's a balancing act. We need to try to attend to both aspects of our lectures as well as we can. Often, our quickest way to gather experience of using the tools in the lecture room is to go there to watch others use them. By sitting in on other people's lectures we can look at what worked well for them, and then go about finding out how to make it work well for us. Equally, and more quietly, we can watch what *didn't* work well for them, and check that we don't fall into the same traps. We hope that this chapter has helped you decide which of the tools of the lecture room can be most helpful to your students – and indeed which you'll get most satisfaction from mastering yourself.

7 What can *students* do in lectures?

What do lecturers expect?

Let's revisit some of the characters we introduced at the start of our book, and look at what they have to say about their expectations of what their students should be doing in their lectures. In fact, it often isn't clear what lecturers expect students to do in lectures; perhaps this is because lecturers tend to be more concerned with what they are teaching than with the experiences of the students during their lectures.

the lecturers ...

Arthur

It's ok for the ones in the front two rows, they can see what I'm showing them. They seem to be the keen ones anyway. It's when I look up to those further back – their faces are blank, they've glazed over. And the ones who aren't interested seem to always sit at the back – and they chatter.

Dr D

I find it very annoying that some of them don't seem to know what they should be doing in my lectures. Some of them sit there vacantly and others wait until I get to the end of a complex worked example and then say, 'Which bits of that were we supposed to write down, then?'

Anya Wilenska

I ask them questions – and they answer. But they drive me insane with their stupid questions to me, they interrupt me all the time and haven't got the courtesy to wait until I have finished my presentation. Is it the students? In my country, you wouldn't look up and see them nodding off! You wouldn't see the ones at the back texting with their mobiles. Can't they see that the slides are just the main points on which I elaborate? It's what I say that they need to be thinking about – but they don't think. Why don't they make notes, these students?

Professor Oakwood

As far as I'm concerned they come to my lectures to get a grip on the subject – or that's what they should be doing. But they expect to be entertained rather than taught and they seem to have very short attention spans. …If I give them all my overheads as they request, they sit there in class doing nothing, so I think it better that they make their own notes.

Dr Arbuthnott

What should my students be doing? Well, as long as they're interested it's enough for me. I adjust what I do using their facial expressions and body language as my barometer. If they don't follow up what was in a lecture and get a grip on it for themselves, there's not a lot I can do about that. The high-fliers don't seem to have a problem with this.

Most lecturers would agree on one thing: students are intended to gain knowledge during their lectures, and to come out of each lecture primed to continue to gain further knowledge by reading, practising, solving problems, talking to each other, asking questions, and so on. In other words, it's about turning information and data into students' knowledge, starting during the lecture and continuing afterwards. Students are meant to come out of each lecture with added value in their minds, and not just additional information in the form of their handouts.

What *do* students do (or expect to do) in lectures?

So what kinds of things do students typically say about what they actually experience in a range of different lecture contexts?

It would be fine if there were 30 of us there, not 130. Things are shown to those at the front, and just never get passed back to us at the back. I can't get there in time to get a seat at the front because I'm in Foster Building for the lecture before this one.

I just can't write that fast. And it's hard to tell what we're supposed to write. The slides go up on the screen, and there's never time to get more than the first two points down before the next slide has appeared. Sometimes we get a printout of all of the slides, and it turns out to be a waste of time trying to write them down in the first place. Other times there's no printout, just when we've been lulled into the security of expecting one and written nothing down. And when I try to make notes, I keep missing points that other people seem to have caught – but they've not made notes, so it's no use trying to catch up with them afterwards. If only they'd tell us exactly what they wanted us to write down, and what to sit and listen and think about.

He asks, 'Any questions?' now and then, but I don't think he really wants them. A student at the back asked one the other day, and she was really put down. 'You weren't listening 10 minutes ago, were you?' he snapped back. Besides, we don't really know what our questions are until we've had time to go through our notes and the handouts together, then half the questions we might have asked are already covered. But then it's too late to ask the questions that are still left over, as he's gone on to a different topic, and he makes it only too obvious that he expects us to have cracked the last one by now.

She tries to get us doing things in groups in the lectures, which would be fine if I had the energy left. It's my third lecture that day and I'm just exhausted. Even when I join in with the people sitting round me, I just feel that they're all keen and awake and I'm desperate for a kip. I'd prefer just to sit and take notes, as at least I can make a reasonable stab at copying things down on autopilot.

I just hate being the one who's picked on when he fires questions at us. It wouldn't be so bad if he asked the question, gave us all a minute or two to think, and then picked on someone who looked as though they had at least something to say. But no, he picks on a person, usually at the end of a row, and then asks them a question. When you're nervous, you can't even make sense of the question, and he has to say it again, and that makes me even more uptight.

What really helps me is that she puts up a slide at the start showing exactly what the lecture is going to contain, and that helps me to see a sort of map of what the lecture is going to cover. She nearly always puts the same slide up near the end, and asks us to raise our hands if we feel we've sorted out each of these outcomes in turn. It makes you think back and join the threads together, and I feel we know where we are with her topics.

His slides are very polished, and we can all see them at the back, but I don't know why he still reads them out so slowly to us all. We can read far faster than he speaks, and we're thinking about the bottom of the slide while he's still talking about the top of it. If he just put one point up at a time it would be better.

I went on a course about 'note-making, not just note-taking', and I'm trying not just to copy things down from what is said or what is put up on the screen. In some lectures it works well, because I can make my notes directly onto the handouts. Sometimes the handouts contain a box for us all to summarize what has been talked about, and we're given a couple of minutes to jot down the gist of our thoughts. This works for me, but my problem is that sometimes while I'm making notes I'm frightened that I'm missing something else.

So what do students take in to lectures? Nowadays it is possible that students will bring laptops, handheld computers or personal organizers with them so they can make notes electronically, but it is still more likely that they bring a pen or pencil, and something to write on. (However, lecturers increasingly tell tales of students arriving at lectures without any means of recording what they hear and see, especially if they are used to being given handouts or being able to access notes from the Web after the lecture.)

More importantly, students take in to lectures their existing knowledge and experience. There will always be at least some of the students who already understand or know most of what is going to be the content of a given lecture. Very few students go in without knowing at least something about what's going to be presented to them. Yet for many students, what they already know or understand still needs to be clarified, adjusted, edited, extended, exemplified, corrected and developed, there and then in the lecture, and afterwards by the students working under their own steam, independently or collaboratively.

Analysing what students do in lectures

If you ask students what they actually *do* during lectures, you'll get a wide range of honest responses. Ask them to focus on *active verbs*, and they'll typically give you all sorts of actions, some with high learning payoff and others with none at all. Here is a selection – in alphabetical order:

Just some of the things students do in lectures

Admiring the cool, calm way the lecturer handles awkward questions.
Being bored.
Being impressed by the way the lecturer makes the technology work.
Catching up with the report that's due in at 11 o'clock.
Chatting to the next student.
Coming down from illegal substances.
Considering dropping out of the course.
Copying things down from the board.
Copying things down from the screen.
Copying things down that the lecturer says (or trying to).
Doing calculations, but then missing other things that are being said.
Feeling desperate for a cigarette.
Feeling embarrassed for the lecturer, standing there struggling away.
Feeling embarrassed that they couldn't answer the question.
Feeling faint.
Feeling put down by the lecturer's response to their answer.
Feeling that they've heard all this before.
Feeling the light dawning – and trying to capture it.
Feeling they are only capturing some of the points.
Feeling too hot.
Fretting about their relationships.
Getting annoyed at the student in front busy texting on a mobile.
Getting excited and wanting to find out more and more about the topic.
Getting hungrier.
Getting really tired.
Highlighting things in the handouts.
Hoping that the cheque has come in the post.
Itching to get to their books to get into the topic deeper.
Jotting down their own answers to the lecturer's questions.
Jotting their notes onto the handout materials.
Listening and thinking, but most of their thoughts being gone again two hours later – or two minutes later sometimes.
Listening to the cricket scores.
Looking for cues about how to tackle the assignment.
Lusting after that student two rows in front.
Making their own notes.
Missing things – while writing down one point, two others have been made that they couldn't get down.

Never getting down as much as they're trying to.

Nodding off.

Still thinking about a previous lecture on a different topic.

Summarizing what's being discussed.

Taking down notes.

Thinking about the cheque that didn't arrive this morning.

Trying not to cough.

Trying to sort out what's important and what's just background.

Trying to stay awake.

Waiting and waiting for some of the class to get things down and for the whole thing to move on.

Waiting for the minutes to go by.

Wanting to leave, but not daring to.

Wanting to talk to their neighbour to check out whether they are the only one who can't see the point.

Watching the lecturer.

Watching the on-screen presentation.

Wishing they hadn't said such-and-such to so-and-so.

Wishing they'd looked at the last two sets of notes, and wondering whether this would have made the present lecture make sense.

Wondering how on earth this person got to be a lecturer.

Wondering if they will dare ask so-and-so out.

Wondering what the lecturer's partner is like.

Working out what seems likely to be coming up in the exam.

Working out where to try to live next.

Worrying about an unwanted pregnancy.

Worrying about the assignment on another module.

Worrying about the credit card demand.

Worrying about whether they will be chucked off the course.

Writing down their own questions so that they can check them out later.

As illustrated here, just about all of life goes on in a crowded lecture room – or even a quite small one. If we were able to have a bank of television monitors at the back of the lecture theatre, each displaying visually what was going on in the minds of separate students at any instant, it would certainly distract us from what we were doing at the front of the theatre!

Some lecturers are not really interested in what the students do in their lectures, in fact they feel it is none of their business. However, most lecturers today recognize that they have some responsibility to promote learning in their lectures. Looking at what lecturers might want their students to be doing in lectures is likely to produce a rather different list (again, alphabetical):

What lecturers might want their students to be doing in lectures

Adding important points to the handouts.

Asking each other questions – and answering each other's questions.

Asking the lecturer questions – and answering the lecturer's questions.

Challenging their assumptions.

Copying down important things from the screen.

Discussing things with each other.

Finding out what others think.

Having complex ideas clarified.

Having misconceptions debunked.

Hearing a range of opinions.

Learning things.

Looking at the visual images on screen and comparing them with works of art seen in exhibitions.

Making additional notes to the handout materials.

Making links with things they had learnt previously.

Making mistakes in buzz group tasks and learning from them.

Making notes.

Picking up my cues about what's important.

Practising things.

Sharing ideas.

Thinking about concepts.

Trying out short problems and getting feedback on how they undertook the task.

Trying to make connections between theory and practice.

Understanding the subject.

Writing down their own questions for later study.

Writing things down.

In short, lecturers' agendas about what students should be doing in lectures tend to be far more focused on the subject, thinking about it, learning it, and so on. Lecturers expect students to be turning the information presented in the lecture into their own knowledge, or (better) adding and integrating the content of the lecture with the knowledge that students bring to the lecture.

Students' minds, however, are likely to remain full of all sorts of wider agendas – that is, unless we can use our teaching skills to make the learning agenda really compelling, so that other things already in students' minds fade into the background.

Keeping attention engaged

We also need to recognize that students' attention spans in lectures can be variable. McKeachie (1994, p57), reviewing the work of Hartley and Davies (1978), indicates that:

> One of the characteristics of a passive lecture situation in which a lecturer is using few devices to get students to think actively about the content of the lecture is that attention tends to drift. Probably all of us have had the experience of listening to a speaker and finding with a start that we have not heard the speaker for some time because our attention has drifted on to thoughts that are tangential to the lecturer's theme. Bloom's (1953) studies of students' thinking during lectures and discussion indicated that more of students' thoughts were relevant to the content during lectures than during discussions, but that there was less active thinking in lectures than in discussions.

He further argues that:

> Studies of the attention of students during lectures find that, typically, attention increases from the beginning of the lecture to ten minutes into the lecture and decreases after that point. They found that after the lecture students recalled 70 percent of the material covered in the first ten minutes, and only 20 percent of the material covered in the last ten minutes. (McKeachie, 1994, p56)

Gibbs (1992, pp113, 114) suggests that attention wanes in lectures after about 15 minutes unless student activity is integrated; many of us recognize this as being true in our own experiences of being students. Often this is symptomatic of a concentration on what is being taught rather than what is being learnt.

What about learning payoff *during* lectures?

One way or another, most people's response to the question, 'What's the point of lectures?' has 'learning' in it somewhere. Students expect to learn something, and lecturers expect them to learn something. It is worth, therefore, exploring some of the things students do in lectures in terms of the likely learning payoff that may result from such actions.

Writing

Most students spend at least some of their time in lectures writing. However, writing in itself is no guarantee of learning taking place. It depends what kinds of writing are involved. Let us therefore go straight into two quite different kinds of writing that happen in lectures – note-*taking* and note-*making*.

Copying things down – taking notes

McKeachie (1994, p59), quoting the research of Hartley and Davies (1978) on note-taking and student information processing during lectures, suggests that:

> Students believe that there are two purposes for taking notes. One is that the process of taking notes will in itself help later recall; the other is that the notes provide external storage of concepts which may be reviewed when needed. The research results indicate some support for both beliefs.

Note-taking certainly keeps students busy and often quiet, but we all know how easy it is for us to copy something down without thinking about it much at all. Sometimes we only begin to think about what we've written down when we read it later.

Just occasionally, we may want students to write down something exactly as we say it or show it on the screen, such as a definition, a mathematical expression, or a short but important quotation from a source. Then we may even 'dictate' the words, and students transcribe them exactly. The problem is that students too often don't really know what they should be doing with the words we say to them and the words on the slides or overheads that we show to them. In this position of uncertainty, the safest thing to do seems to be to try to 'capture' the words by copying them down. 'Well, at least I've got what was being talked about written down, so I'll have a good chance to be able to work out what it all means in due course', students may naturally think. But all too often, weeks later, they read what they've written down and it makes no sense to them at all. There's no longer the tone of voice, the body language of the lecturer, the emphasis on certain words, the speed and all the other things that make it easier to understand what it really means.

In short, copying things down more often than not delivers little learning payoff. That said, we often don't ever *intend* students to copy things down in the first place. We may be going to give the words themselves out in handout materials, or printouts of the slides, or files on the Web that they can download, play with and add to. Or the words may already be there in handout materials right in front of the students' eyes. And then, it's only human nature for students to switch off mentally: 'No point in spending energy on words I already have in my handouts', they may think (Bligh 2000a).

Note-taking is therefore, on the whole, a tenuous activity in terms of learning payoff. What about note-*making*?

Making notes

This is what most lecturers would actually *like* students to be doing in lectures – not just copying things down, but *processing* what's being shown and said, and turning it into their own notes. However, getting students to *make* notes is an uphill struggle for many reasons, including:

- It's simply much easier to take notes than to make notes. Especially when students are tired, or even bored, simply capturing the words (or numbers, diagrams and everything else they see and hear) is relatively straightforward.
- Taking notes give students a sense that they're doing their bit; it seems much better than just sitting thinking about what the lecturer is trying to say.
- It seems like a sensible insurance policy, trying to 'capture' the lecture so that there's more chance of being able to get to grips with the content later.
- *Making* notes has more risks associated with it, especially of being so busy putting down the *sense* of what's just been covered, that the next bit gets missed entirely.
- Students often don't know exactly when we would *expect* them to be making notes rather than just taking them.
- Students sometimes don't feel that they know *how* to make good notes.

If we stop and think about exactly what students *can* actually be doing when they're making notes, their actions can include:

- Making decisions about what's important enough to write down, and what's just background detail.
- Annotating what's already in the handout materials in front of them, to help the handouts reflect the emphasis that the lecturer is giving at the time.
- Writing down questions that may be worth following up later.
- Capturing passing thoughts and reactions to what's being discussed or presented, to follow up later, or ignore as necessary.
- Jotting down instances where the light has just dawned on an idea or concept, to remind them of the thinking that has just happened, and help them to recapture it again later.
- Jotting down questions that other students have just asked, and which seem worth remembering, and being able to answer in future.
- Putting things in order of priority, for example if there are seven bullet points in a list of 'causes' in the handout, working out which of these are the most important ones to think about in future.
- Jotting down 'for and against' arguments, to help to fill out the picture of a debate or discussion during the lecture.
- Making decisions about which of the sources the lecturer is mentioning are going to be the most important ones to follow up after the lecture.
- Gathering clues from the lecturer's words and actions about exactly what may be expected in related coursework assignments or future exam questions.
- Working out what the intended learning outcomes, which may have been presented at the start of the lecture, printed on the handout or listed in the course documentation, actually *mean* in terms of the evidence students will be expected to furnish in due course of having achieved these outcomes.
- Turning the 'linear' picture presented in the printed handout into a flow diagram, concept map, or something else that shows how the separate elements fit together, overlap, and link to each other.

As can be seen from the list above, all of these activities involve a great deal more *thinking* than just transcribing the content of the lecture. In other words, these more strenuous activities cumulatively add up to much higher learning payoff for students. While we may hope that students would work all this out for themselves, we are only too aware sometimes that while the most able students have already done so, many of their fellow students have not, or can not, or would like to but don't know how.

There are indeed some things that lecturers can do to help students to make notes rather than take them. These include:

- Stopping for a few minutes now and then in a lecture, and briefing students to 'make' notes. For example: 'Use the next three minutes to jot down for yourself the three most important things that we've been thinking about' and then, 'Spend a minute or two comparing what *you've* written with what the people on either side of you have just written, and add their best ideas to yours.'
- Sharing with students the differences between note-taking and note-making, and asking them to help in making sure that they did indeed get assistance and encouragement to make notes during lectures.
- Asking students to jot down their own thoughts or ideas about the issue to be addressed next in a lecture, and spending a minute or two letting students share these thoughts, before going on with the lecture, allowing students to pick up those of their own ideas which proved to be most relevant.
- Using handouts that have plenty of free space for students to make notes around what's already there, and which reduce the temptation to take notes by already containing the wording of key slides.
- Adding boxes to handouts, with task briefings to allow students to get straight into making decisions and working out priorities at the same time as (or shortly after) things are being presented or discussed in the lecture.
- Encouraging students to take risks with note-making, and then follow up the lecture by comparing each other's notes, and adding to them things that may have been missed as a result of concentrating on making notes rather than just taking them.

It can also be well worth referring students to the extensive study-skills literature (some of which is listed in the 'References and further reading' at the back of this book) which will be readily available to them in libraries or learning resources centres, and indicating to them the discussions of note-making most relevant to the topics and disciplines in the lecture course.

Asking questions

This is an activity with at least some potential for high learning payoff – the person who asks the question is likely to learn something. Even just *thinking* of questions to ask is a useful activity, but can evaporate into nothing unless the questions – and the answers – are jotted down at the time.

Opening up a lecture to 'any questions' serves some purposes, but has several disadvantages, including:

- It tends to be the more confident students who ask questions in front of a large group of their peers, and they aren't necessarily the ones who most need to find out the answers to the questions.
- While the student who has asked a question is usually quite eager to find out the answer, other students may know it already, and others may not care about it.
- The questions tend to come in rather slowly, and in random order.
- Students often perceive it as a prompt to pack up their books and papers prior to leaving.

We can, however, do a lot as lecturers to encourage a great deal more question asking in our lectures. Things we can do include:

- Encouraging students, while they are making notes, to continuously seek to annotate them with questions that are passing through their minds at any moment, for example using a different coloured pen to put several question marks beside a word or idea that they don't yet understand. Even if most of the passing questions are resolved in the next few minutes of the lecture, it remains useful for students to see in their notes this record of their transient thinking, and they can continue to check out that they do now indeed understand the answers to those questions.
- Pausing in the lecture, and asking all students to jot down three things they don't yet know about what has been discussed in the last few minutes, then allowing them to ask each other their questions. Most will be answered quite readily by fellow students talking to each other, but some of the outstanding questions can then be redirected back to the lecturer to respond to.
- Asking students in groups to jot down questions they'd like answered, writing them on Post-its or slips of paper, and passing them down to the lecturer, who can pick out ones to answer immediately and retain the rest to cover important or frequently asked ones later, or in the next lecture.
- Asking students in clusters to generate some 'possible exam questions' based on the last lecture or two, and jot them down on overhead transparency slips, and send them down to the front. Lecturers can then show and comment on the questions, for example giving feedback along the lines, 'This one would be too long for

a half-hour exam question' or, 'This one would be rather too easy' or, 'This one is bang on the sort of thing which you should be able to do', and so on.

In these ways, the learning payoff associated with asking questions can be increased and shared among students, even when in large lecture groups.

Answering questions

This has obvious learning payoff for students. Asking individuals questions in lectures has limits, in that with a large group even with frequent questions from the lecturer, only a few students are directly caused to find out to what extent they really are able to answer the questions asked – those students actually asked for their responses to the questions. However, asking the whole group to think about the answer to a question, then pausing, then choosing one or more respondents, causes more thinking to be done, as few students want to be without something they could say in response if they happen to be picked.

Students may indeed try to avoid being picked, for example by avoiding eye contact at the crucial moment. One way to randomize questioning of this sort is to write numbers (for example, 1 to 176) on the top right-hand corner of the front page of students' handout materials, and alert students that this has been done and ask them to note their number, and (more important) the numbers of people immediately beside them. Then a question can be posed, a pause given, and then you can pick a number at random: 'Who's got 134, please?' The owners of particular numbers may try to conceal their identity, but students beside them almost always enjoy giving the game away. Once students realize that their number could come up at any moment, the whole group thinks much harder of answers during the pauses, and the learning payoff from quizzing the group increases quite dramatically. However, you will need to be sensitive to the fact that some students for personal or cultural reasons may feel oppressed by being called upon to speak up in front of their peers and to back off if a student is genuinely unwilling to answer.

Handouts can be really useful to increase the learning payoff associated with answering questions. A list of open-ended questions in part of a handout is much more effective at prompting activity than merely providing the answers. The questions can be used as prompts during the lecture, with students making notes as the answers to the questions arise during the lecture. When students already have questions planted in their minds, they are much more receptive as the answers are revealed. Indeed, students may, if given the chance, often have a try at answering the questions themselves first, by sketching in guesses in their handout materials, then checking which proved to be correct or not as the discussion develops, especially if handouts are available in advance as part of a learning support package or on the Web.

Handouts can also be used to help students to gather together what they already know from previous lectures, in the first few minutes of the next one. For example, if the first page of a handout has a series of short, sharp revision questions, the class can be given five minutes for everyone to jot down their answers to these questions, and members of the group can be selected to speak out their individual answers. Even students who are relatively reluctant to speak out in front of the large group may feel more comfortable doing so when they have already jotted down their answers, and the process becomes one with a high learning payoff for most of the group. A few minutes spent in this way at the start of a lecture can also be a way of minimizing the inconvenience caused by latecomers – who soon find that they have missed something relatively useful and may be less likely to be late next time.

Similarly, towards the end of a lecture, it can be useful to have another question-and-answer episode, based on questions already in the handout materials, or on a separate sheet given out at that stage. Telling students that all of the questions cumulatively mount up to letting them know exactly what they are expected to be able to handle in forthcoming exam questions can help them to think about using the handouts more actively as revision aids, rather than just providing information to learn.

Since much of the assessment of students' progress is based, in one way or another, on them becoming better able to answer questions with precision, speed and depth, the high level of learning payoff associated with embracing the question–answer process during lectures is obvious, and the benefits of making the process transparent by using printed questions in handouts are clear.

Explaining things to each other

The act of explaining something to someone else invariably has high learning payoff. The person explaining it gets a stronger grip on it simply through the process of putting it into words and communicating it to someone else. Indeed, as lecturers, we continue to deepen our own understanding of our subjects by explaining things to our students. But we can share the benefits with students by getting *them* to explain things to each other.

For example, in a maths lecture, imagine the moment when about a third of the students can understand what the lecturer has just demonstrated, and the other two-thirds haven't yet 'seen the light'. We can ask for a show of hands from those students for whom the light has now dawned, and check out by a further show of hands that for the remainder they're not yet there. Then asking each of the students who *can* understand it to explain to two or three of those who can't, can deliver really high learning payoff. Logistically, this may cause one or two problems where the 'illuminated' students are sitting together in the same part of the tiered auditorium, but benefits accrue when those who are doing the explaining deepen their own understanding by putting the idea across to those who didn't understand it.

In turn, the students who are struggling benefit from having it explained to them by someone who has just seen how to do it – while it is fresh in their minds. Someone who has just found out something is in the best possible position to explain it to others, as they can still remember exactly how the light dawned. For us lecturers, it is often far harder to explain some difficult things to students, as we can't remember how it felt when we first began to understand it ourselves. We sometimes can't even imagine *not* being able to understand something – we've known it for so long.

The learning payoff associated with a theatre-full of students explaining key points or having them explained to them can be enormous – well worth us passing the session over to the students for a few minutes at a time when an appropriately important or tricky concept or idea comes into play.

Handouts for learning, not just for information

We've already touched on the idea that handout materials used in lectures don't just have to be summaries of the information we wish students to take away with them to learn later. When handout materials are turned into interactive learning materials, they cause far more learning payoff to be delivered. In particular, when handouts are full of things for students to *do*, during and after lectures, they become a much more valuable resource than just yet more information. When students do a lot of writing onto their handout materials (answering questions on them, brainstorming their own ideas, filling in brief summaries of what has been discussed, and so on), they value the handouts much more. You can see the difference in the way they keep them carefully and organize them in their folders. Handouts into which students have committed a fair amount of thinking are seldom seen as paper aeroplanes or in bins around the campus!

There is no escaping the fact that preparing handouts designed to be learning resource materials for students takes more time than simply providing them with summaries of the content of a lecture. More paper may also be needed, not least because of the blank space for students to do things with the tasks in the handouts. The costs are therefore higher too. However, well-designed interactive handouts reap benefits for lecturers as well as for students. For a start, they are direct evidence of the intended quality of the learning–teaching interactions we are trying to achieve through our lectures. They are not seen as just a duplication of information that students could have found for themselves outside the lecture, or downloaded from the intranet, and so on. When students find the handouts really valuable *during* as well as after lectures, problems with lecture attendance can diminish remarkably. It is then no substitute just photocopying someone else's handout after a missed lecture. Indeed, students who have invested quite a lot of their own thinking into their copy of an interactive handout may be somewhat reluctant to give theirs to a friend to copy in case it gets lost. The extra time and cost that go into producing handouts of this nature can be well justified in terms of providing our students with *learning* resources rather than simply providing ourselves with teaching aids.

If we're intent on turning handout materials into learning resources, it is natural enough to make sure that each handout helps to paint the picture of what we really expect our students to be doing in their learning, not only through the level of the tasks and exercises contained in the handouts themselves, but by using the handouts to present to the students the associated specific intended learning outcomes directly associated with each particular lecture in the programme. It can also be useful to add some printed briefing notes to help students to understand what these learning outcomes actually mean for them in terms of the standards they should be aiming to reach as they continue to work with the subject matter addressed by the handouts, as they revise and prepare for summative assessments such as exams. When students learn a great deal from *using* their handout materials, and see them as a unifying thread running through a programme of lectures, we find out very quickly that they are indeed being valued, from students' feedback responses about a course in general. This positive feedback is of course a very welcome dimension of the evidence we have that our lectures themselves are being well received.

What else can lecturers do in lectures to help keep students focused and attentive?

If we want to keep students with us over periods of an hour or longer, conventional wisdom (as well as the research cited by McKeachie above) suggests that we need to build in a variety of attention recall points to stop their attention from drifting away from the topic of the lecture. The consultant team who worked with Gibbs on the PCFC-funded 'Teaching more students' project (Gibbs, 1992, pp13–31) came up with a range of suggestions, (in addition to the use of questions and answers and handouts), which we have summarized and expanded upon here:

- *Give the students a break*, in the form of an actual rest for a few moments, an invitation to read their own or a colleagues' notes, to have a stretch, to tackle a problem, to silently reflect or to plan future work associated with a topic.
- *Get them to read a short section of a handout*, on the premise that it changes the activity, but also enables some fast coverage of material that can be unpacked in a later part of the lecture (although we offer caveats here about over-use, especially where students with visual impairments or dyslexia are present).
- *Get some instant feedback on how they are doing*, perhaps by a show of hands, instant questionnaire, Post-it exercise or by electronic means.
- *Undertake some kind of mini-assessment task* like a quiz, a set of multi-task questions on screen, or a short written test on the handout.
- *Change the nature of the stimulus:* for example, if the students have been looking at slides in the dark, put the main lights on and talk without reference to images for a while, or if the main technique up to that point has been talking through a PowerPoint presentation, give them a single image or video clip to look at for a moment.
- *Change the activity:* if the students have been writing solidly for 20 minutes or more, you could ask them just to sit and listen to you or an audio clip for a few minutes without writing anything down. If they have been following your explanation or exposition for a while, asking them individually or in pairs to apply the concept to a problem provides variety.

Conclusion

In this chapter we've been exploring the learning which students can achieve *during* lectures, and seeing that in fact there is a great deal that we ourselves can do to increase the learning payoff that our lectures actually deliver, right there in the lecture room, to students. We want, of course, for the learning not to stop the moment that students walk out of a lecture. Nor is it wise for us to base our hopes on students' learning *beginning* after they walk out of a lecture! If we put the time we have with the students to good effect in getting them started on their learning, they are much more likely to continue spontaneously after a lecture. It's often the energy it takes to *start* learning something that can be the hurdle that really needs to be overcome, and we can help students to make a start by getting them learning as a normal part of being in our lectures, not just showing them *what* they should learn later.

8 Before and after lectures

We'll start this chapter with some of the things that lecturers do before and after lectures – and then think about some of the things they *could* do, which may help make their lectures a better learning experience for students. Then we'll look at what lecturers think *students* should do before and after lectures, and suggest some advice that can be given to them to help to retain and make sense of the lecture material.

What do lecturers do before their lectures?

Most of us check the timetable to make sure we're going to the right room and seeing the right class (although there are anecdotes in most institutions relating to those few occasions when one or both of these activities got missed out!) We visit the facilities and check in the mirror that we're fit for students to look at. We head off for the venue in reasonable time, and try not to stop and talk to people on the way there. 'Catch you later, but I'm on in Theatre 5 next' we say, purposefully.

What about preparing for the event itself?

the lecturers ...

Dr D

Having checked what's on the course programme, I concentrate on getting the materials together. I do my preparation before each lecture. I go through my papers and abstracts and choose the ones I'm going to be referring to in the lecture. I get copies made for handouts. I make sure I know which pages of the reader I'm going to link things to. Sometimes I find that I have prepared far too much, but if I don't get through it all, I just refer them to the Web pages.

Professor Oakwood

I would say I've got it all sorted out by now. I've given the course often enough. I hardly need my notes any more, but I have a quick look at them before most lectures, if only to remind myself where I'm starting off from. Compared to my research, the lecture course is just the basics, so I don't have to do much more than remind myself of which topic I'm doing in the particular lecture.

Bill

I prepare my script for ages, adjusting what I used last time for each new lecture. I print it large so I can see it easily even when the lights are down for slides. Days ahead, I mentally run through it, timing myself to see if I've got enough there. Then I have to work out what I could cut out to get through it in 50 minutes. But I speak faster when I get nervous, so this can backfire. Then I start worrying and fretting. Each lecture is quite an ordeal for me. I sometimes just wish I could put it out of my mind, and go for a walk around the campus for some fresh air. But that doesn't really help, and I end up back at my desk again, looking at the script and checking and checking it.

Dr Arbuthnott

No one could do more. I spend time getting the handouts right, straight from my latest version of the PowerPoint slides (minus the video clips and Web links of course – but they're referenced in the handouts so students can find them again). I get into Theatre 3 first thing in the day for any of my big-group lectures – the porter knows me well by now and opens the room for me as soon as he sees me coming. Most times everything works fine, but if there's a problem the technician's always not far away, and we crack it between us.

Louise

There's never enough time: 11 o'clock is always upon me before I'm quite ready. I collect bits and pieces that I might use for weeks sometimes, and make overheads while I think of things that could be useful. The reprographics people are rushed off their feet in the middle of term, so I can't always get handouts done till later, but as long as students get them before they start revising, it doesn't matter too much.

Most lectures last for an hour or less, but for most of us they take much larger bites out of our days – a one-hour lecture at 11 am can be a morning gone. After all, it's not just that we give lectures. We have research to do, reading to keep up with, student work to mark, exams to set, meetings to attend, paperwork to organize and file, handouts to prepare, overheads or slides to prepare, sort and file, and so on. It's a wonder we actually have time to give lectures!

When you talk to many lecturers about preparing their lectures, they often mention issues relating to the content, which of course is extremely important. Less often, they talk about how they are going to put the material across to students.

So when it comes to what do we do *before* a lecture, it's hardly surprising that the responses of most lecturers, particularly new ones, are geared to survival – trying to make sure that the event will go off without hitches. The problem is that we tend to instinctively focus before lectures on things that relate to *our* comfort levels, trying to avoid embarrassment and tension. Because of this, it's easy to get sidetracked from the real reason for having lectures – learning. In other words, we instinctively concentrate on 'getting our act together', when perhaps we should be adding to this a lot more about 'getting *their* act together'.

So what *could* we do before our lectures?

Essentially, preparing a lecture can be about many overlapping things, including those listed below (but let's say at once that this is a shopping list of possibilities, and we can seldom afford the time to do all of them as well as we might wish):

- Planning and preparing what students will have in their hands (or on their screens) before, during and after the lecture – the handouts, Web pages, and so on.
- Working out exactly where that particular lecture fits in to the bigger picture of the course or module, so that we can help students to use it as part of their route mapping.
- Thinking about how to actually *start* the lecture, even though there may still be some students who haven't yet arrived, but conscious of the impatience of the punctual should we keep them sitting idly for more than a little while.
- Choosing how to link the present lecture to the last one, and how to tune students back in to the thinking that we aimed to have them doing on that last occasion, and extend it to the agenda to follow.
- Deciding exactly what the learning payoff for students *during* the lecture is meant to be – what the intended learning outcomes are, which students should have achieved by five-to-the-hour.

- Planning how we're going to manage *our* time, and *students'* time during the 50 minutes or so, to allow some flexibility for matters arising, students' questions, our own inspirations or anecdotes, and all the other things that can happen during the session.
- Thinking about how best to use tone of voice, emphasis, repetition, body language and facial expression to bring to the occasion all those things that are not easily captured in resource materials.
- Thinking about how we can do three things at the same time: stretch and stimulate those students for whom the lecture content is plainly straightforward, avoid terminally demoralizing those students who are very stretched, and keep those students in between usefully engaged.
- Leaving ourselves room to cope with the unexpected, so that we don't feel we have to brush aside questions that need addressing there and then, or responding to puzzled or passive expressions on students' faces.
- Working out what students should be briefed to do *after* the lecture, to achieve the remainder of the learning outcomes associated with that particular lecture.
- Thinking through how best to bring the lecture to a definite conclusion, rather than just being caught in mid-flow by the sound of the next set of students outside the door.

In short, most of the actions in the list above relate primarily to student learning processes, and the effect of these on our own teaching performances. The time before a lecture can be well spent by running through the learning pathway that we intend our students to navigate. The danger is, that because *we* know that pathway only too well, we can easily overestimate how much students are likely to learn as we proceed through the lecture.

What about *after* a lecture?

the lecturers ...

Arthur

It's straight back to the studio for me. Often two or three of the students will come along with me, if they haven't another lecture straightaway, and we sit down and brew up some coffee and chat. I often feel that this is where the real learning starts. If only I could explain things in the same way in the lectures themselves, but it just doesn't work like that. I sometimes feel guilty that the students who come along are getting a better deal than the students who don't, but that's the way it happens.

Dr D

I'm catching up with my postgrads – they know it's a good time to catch me after a lecture. They ambush me. At least it helps me to put the lecture out of the mind, when it's one that hasn't gone brilliantly.

Professor Oakwood

Well I'm only too pleased to spend a couple of minutes with those students who come up and ask the odd question. I usually know where to send them off to for more information. But then I'm usually already minutes late for a committee or Faculty Board and so on, so I tell them I'll pick up the matter in the next session.

Bill

I try to forget it for a while – I just want to think about something else! I try to make sure that I've got practice examples of anything that seemed to be a problem for the students, so that I can make a good job of it with them in the problems classes.

Louise

It's such a relief to get back to my research. I'm only lecturing for a few hours most weeks, but it doesn't half mess up my week.

In an ideal world, many lecturers can think of really useful things they might have done soon after a particular lecture, while it was still fresh in their minds, but life in universities and colleges takes its toll, and they are all too easily caught up in all the other things awaiting their attention. For some, indeed, 60 minutes in a lecture theatre, with no phone calls, no e-mails, and no knocks on the door are a welcome relief from the hurly-burly of academic life. A luxury!

Encouraging post-lecture reflection

In most institutions, new lecturers working towards awards such as the Postgraduate Certificate in Academic Practice, are invariably encouraged to follow up their lectures quite consciously and deliberately, and to collect *evidence* of how they reflected upon it, adjusted it for next time, learnt from the things that may have not gone too well, building on things which went really well, and so on. Ask lecturers what it means to be 'a reflective practitioner' and many will recall this sort of meta-analysis that can be done after any lecture. However, new lecturers working towards an award are most likely to undertake follow-up analysis of a few particular lectures, and collect their thoughts and reflections carefully because someone is going to look at them and assess their reflections or accredit their evidence. What happens when that sort of external pressure is off? What happens when there are 7 or 27 lectures in the average week?

Following up lectures amid a busy schedule involving many other things, has to be brought back to the art of the possible. What can we do, realistically, within a day or two? More importantly, what can we do which will save us time and energy in the long run? Here is another shopping list, and again it has to be for individuals to decide which items will be most suitable for them, in their own contexts.

Annotate the artefacts

In the process of giving a lecture, many potential adjustments come to mind – far too many sometimes to remember even a week later. For example, spelling and punctuation errors are found in handout materials, often as a result of students' questions or comments. The danger is that the same errors just aren't noticed a week later, and perhaps a year later the same errors remain in the same handouts. Immediately after a lecture, it only takes a minute or two with a brightly coloured pen to annotate a copy of the handout material, marking it up so that such things can be put right or added. At the same time, there are usually a few things worth noting down to add to the handout for next time round – for example addressing a point which confused some students. There are often things worth noting to delete from the handout next time round too, perhaps a reference that has just been superseded.

Similarly, it's worth annotating overheads. While we may not want to write clumsily onto carefully prepared desktop-published full-colour acetates, it takes seconds to stick Post-its onto the words or bullet points that could usefully be adjusted for next time, indicating briefly the exact adjustments to be made in due course. In any case, when using acetates that have been produced using an inkjet printer, writing on them with overhead pens is likely to render them useless as the solvents in the pen ink get to work on the surface coating of the acetate and make the print run!

With PowerPoint presentations, it's much easier to make adjustments really quickly. It's well worth finding five minutes to run again through the sequence, this time in 'edit' frame of mind, first having saved '216 Kinetics 1' as '216 Kinetics 1a' for example, so that the original is still safe if one messes up the editing. At least the software keeps track of the respective dates for us, so months later we can easily remind ourselves which is the most recent version. This can be the time to attend straightaway to that slide which people at the back complained they couldn't see – spread it out over two slides, adjust the colours or font sizes, and so on.

Then there's our own script or 'annotated agenda': the notes we may have used as prompts about the sequence we used, the task briefings we used for buzz group activities, and the optional activities we planned in case there was time, all deserve revisiting. A year later, we're unlikely to remember the activities we *did* use from those we *might have* used, and so on. It's worth having a different coloured pen to quickly mark up the script or notes with some key reminders about what we actually did, and our immediate thoughts about what we might well try next time. 'This didn't work' can save us doing it again. 'They liked this' is a useful note for the future. 'This got them going' is even better.

Making these adjustments while they are fresh in our minds is far more efficient than sitting down later and trying to remember what we were thinking about. It saves us time. It also saves us confusion – even a week later it's easy to get mixed up between what went well in one lecture and what went well in another, and so on. When you give the same (or a very similar) lecture several times to different groups of students in the same week (or even semester) it can be difficult to keep track of what you said to whom. This is a case where five minutes' worth of notes can keep you on the ball, and when relying on memory just doesn't work. So, having annotated our artefacts, what next?

Files, not piles (a counsel of perfection)!

Another time-saving dimension of post-lecture activity can be the seconds it takes to put all the artefacts into a cardboard wallet or plastic slipcase. This includes a copy of the handout, the overheads, a disk containing just that PowerPoint file, not all the rest, and so on – disks are cheap. Having the whole set of presentations on our laptop or desktop computer is fine, but there's nothing like having the particular one in just the right place (for when the larger machines inevitably crash or are replaced). Even if the contents of the file will be needed again for reference during the next lecture, it's still useful that they're in their separate place, properly indexed, and returned to that place. It's then just *one* thing for us to pick up and take along, rather than a sorting and searching job.

Colour coding can help – cardboard wallets come in several colours. Sticky labels are even cheaper, help with re-using cardboard wallets, and stick well to plastic slipcases, annotated using different coloured pens to make them easy to identify and find. For those who really *enjoy* being organized, you can get nine-part dividers – a sort of large, indexed scrapbook into which you can insert the paperwork for the next few things in your week, including the folders with the 11 am and 3 pm lectures today, along with the committee papers for the 1 pm meeting (keeping perhaps the final section for 'must do today' tasks, and the penultimate one for 'should do this week' tasks).While it is possible for organizing and filing to become displacement activities, if kept to sensible boundaries they can save hours. More importantly, being organized certainly saves minutes, allowing you to spend some of these on what comes next…

Reflection

You might argue that reflection took place while the artefacts were being marked up. But that didn't necessary *capture* the reflection entirely. Gibbs (1998b) argues: 'It is the way you as a teacher actively explore the meaning and implications of feedback which produces the positive results.' It's often useful to prepare yourself a single prompt-sheet or pro-forma to use for a few minutes within a few hours of each and every lecture. You can print these out on a particular colour of paper, so that you can easily find them again (and to remind you to fill one in each time). They can be the front sheet or the back sheet in the cardboard wallet or plastic slipcase for the lecture. Everyone has their own way of reflecting, and Chapter 11 on using feedback develops this further, but as a start, a useful prompt on which to base your reflection might be a series of questions. Here are some from which you might choose a personal selection:

- What was the best thing I did in that lecture?
- What will I try to avoid next time I do this?
- What surprised me?
- Was there too much for me to get through, or too little, or just right?

- What important questions did students ask?
- What did I ask the students, which worked well?
- What couldn't they answer? And why not?
- What did they get muddled or confused about?
- Did I feel rushed at the end?
- Did it work, showing the students the intended outcomes at the start, and reminding them of them at the end? If not, how could I tackle this?
- What did I learn about the class as a whole from this lecture?
- What did I find out about particular students from this lecture?
- What did I learn about my own grasp of the subject from this lecture?
- What did I learn about my technique from this lecture?
- Were there any particular difficulties that I didn't anticipate?

Ideally, once you've decided on the agenda that will be most useful for your own reflection prompt-sheet, it's best that the prompts fit onto only one side of A4 paper, so that you can scan back at your reflections on a given lecture in a single eyeful. The other side can be for explanatory or continuation notes, asterisked from the front side, but only when needed.

If you turn 'reflection' into a doable, manageable, efficient task, it's far more likely that you will build it into your routine. It might be far smaller in scale than the follow-up you may have done on that Postgraduate Certificate programme, but it is much more important that it's ongoing and useful, rather than a good idea abandoned.

From time to time...

There are several things that can cause deep and useful reflection now and then, but which can't possibly be built in as routine for every lecture. These include:

- Using peer observation and feedback: we cover this in Chapter 11 in more detail. Many institutions plan for this as a regular or inter-mittent way of allowing lecturers to learn from each other. Perhaps the most advantageous of such schemes are those that focus on 'classroom observation' rather than just 'peer observation' – in other words where your observer is concentrating on what your *students* seem to be making of the session, rather than just on what you are doing.
- Talking to someone with expertise in the area of learning and teaching in HE. Gibbs (1998b) argues that:

While simply obtaining student feedback has been found to lead to some improvement, what really makes a difference is sitting down with someone who can help you to interpret the feedback and to decide what to do in response to it... It is the way you as a teacher actively explore the meaning and implications of feedback which produces the positive results.

- Looking at a video of yourself in action. We all find out things about ourselves from seeing ourselves perform, that we would not have been able to find out in any different way. Sometimes we can learn significant things from a short video clip. Sometimes it's painful to watch or listen to ourselves. But we tend to be our own worst critics, and seeing our mannerisms or peculiarities on-screen can often irritate us beyond belief, when the same things are just taken as normal by students. There's nothing better, of course, than having a camera-person in your lecture now and again, zooming in to your slides, swivelling round to capture students' faces, and so on. But then it becomes contrived, and even off-putting for most lecturers. A single still camera set up by you or a student at the start, or a self-controlled set-up as used at the University of Derby through the VESOL project, which allows lecturers to control cameras from the front console, can give you really useful visual and other feedback about what you are doing.
- Don't forget audio-tape as a means of facilitating self-analysis. Even just *hearing* snippets of how your lecture went can be a useful aid to reflection, particularly for question-and-answer episodes. Making audio-tapes can also be invaluable for students whose first language is not the language in use or those with visual impairments or dyslexia.

What do lecturers want *students* to do before and after lectures?

the lecturers ...

Chorus: Professor Oakwood, Dr D, Salima, Louise, Anya (and others)

Well, it's obvious isn't it? They should come prepared. They should have processed the last lecture, followed up the references, and had a go at any tasks which we set or suggested in the last lecture. They should bring to a lecture the further learning they have since achieved through tutorials, seminars, practical work, and so on. They should bring with them at least the notes they made from the last lecture, and any other relevant bits and pieces they did since then.

They should still be able to do all the things that they learnt to do from previous lectures, so that they can add to them and extend them with what's going to be presented in the next lecture.

They should know from the programme what the next lecture is about, and should have done some reading around so that it won't all be new to them and wash over their heads. After all, we usually tell them what we expect them to do between particular lectures, either orally or in the handouts.

And after the lecture they should continue in the same way. We can't do their learning for them, least of all in a lecture. *They* are the ones heading for the exams. A few 50-minute lectures won't get them through those. We all remind students all the time that it's a full-time job being a student – a 60-hour week at least. We know that some of them have to work as well to stay in higher education, but they can still be *thinking* about the course while they're stacking shelves or serving burgers.

This kind of concerted response illustrates views that are quite frequently heard. First, the onus is on students to come prepared to lectures, and to have followed up previous lectures – in short, to be managing their own learning between lectures. Second, this expectation is obvious to students – far too obvious to need spelling out to them.

Students, however, may tell many different stories about the 'before and after' agenda.

students' views ...

Most of our lecturers give us 'suggested reading' between lectures. What speed do these people read at? It must be measured in pages per second! Or at least that's what they seem to think that we can do. No way! If we were to try to do it all, we'd be reading day and night – and that would mean we wouldn't be taking much in. They seem to think that their subject is the only one we're studying, and they give us all this stuff to read, one after another. It wouldn't be so bad if they said to us, 'If you only have time to read two things, these are the two to go for...'

We get reading lists in the Module Handbooks – masses of them. But quite often, most of the stuff on the lists is never even mentioned by the lecturers. Why is all this stuff on the lists? Have the lecturers ever read some of it? Or is it just there to make the Handbooks look good? Are some of the references just there to give an impression of 'quality'? And do they just refer to their own books to make sure we buy them and push up their royalties?

One of our lecturers uses a core text. This is good in that we know exactly where the majority of the material is coming from – especially useful when you have to skip a lecture to go to the dentist. We're also asked to read through specific sections before each particular lecture, and the lecturer picks us at random and asks short questions to find out whether we have or not. It keeps us on our toes – you don't want to be the one who hasn't a clue when such questions land on us.

I like it when they give out task sheets at the end of a lecture, and a 'mark it yourself' sheet at the end of the next lecture. If you have a go at the tasks, you can find out for yourself whether you're up to scratch. Some people cheat of course, and just collect the questions and answers and save them for revision. However, I always have a go, and it's good to find out things I've got wrong without anyone looking over my shoulder. That makes me more relaxed about learning from my mistakes.

Two of our lecturers don't give us any work between lectures. They say, 'It's up to you to find your feet, I'm just highlighting *some* bits of the syllabus, but your exam will be on *all* of the syllabus.' This doesn't seem fair. How are we expected to know the level of the questions we can expect in those areas that the lecturers haven't gone through?

They give out work in lectures for us to have a go at, and bring along to the tutorials. The problem is if you haven't had a go at the work, the easiest thing is just to skip the tutorials – saves embarrassment! I've every intention of catching up on all this work when I really get down to revision, but at the moment every spare minute is spent writing up lab reports, because they won't assign you with another experiment until the last-but-one is handed in.

It's all very well to be told to 'Read Chapter 3 of Simpson and Watkins as preparation for next week's session' – but there's 50-odd pages there. One of our lecturers has a better way, and gives out a sheet with about 20 short questions, and says, 'Scan through Chapter 5 of Bloggs, just looking for the answers to these questions – I'll quiz you all on them at the start of next week's session.' That works for me, I'm getting good at speed reading, looking for answers. This has actually helped me get better at other sorts of reading too – I pay a lot more attention now to the contents pages and indexes, and look for things in books and articles rather than just sitting there reading them.

What about after each lecture? They just seem to assume that once *they've* covered it, we've got it in our heads for ever. It wasn't like that with Critical Theory. I could see what he was getting at during the lecture, but that's three weeks ago now. I look at the notes and it just doesn't make sense any more. I wish I'd got a video of the lecture, maybe then I could play it again and again to keep it in my mind. It's no use setting essays on it to be handed in at the tutorial if no-one can do them.

One lecturer gives us a one-page summary of all the important points. This seems a good idea, but the temptation is not to make notes during the lectures, and just rely on the summary. Also, I dug out the summaries for the first six lectures, and tried to answer one of last year's exam questions just from these – I got thoroughly stuck, until I dug into the textbooks for lots more detail.

It's hardly cool to be seen to be diving into all the work they give us straight away – plenty of people just aren't doing it. It's only November now and the exam isn't till June in this Module, so it will all work out in the end. I'm putting my energy into the two Modules that finish at Christmas first.

One lecturer gives the whole class a short spot test every three weeks or so – just 10 minutes, sitting there in the lecture theatre, and answering a series of questions that are put up on the screen. The tests don't count, but our answers are taken in after the 10 minutes, with our names on them. He comes in next week and plays war with us about the silly mistakes we're making. But he does go over the main things that we got wrong, so I suppose that's useful.

It's no use them going on about the 60-hour week we're supposed to be doing to be safe at the end-of-year exams, or threatening us that only two-thirds of us will be back next year, on average. That just depresses us. I'm knackered half the time I'm in lectures because I've been up in the early hours with my two-year-old. Something's got to give. It's ok for those with no responsibilities, but what can the rest of us do? One of my friends has a mother who's terminally ill, and even when she's got time to do things, she just can't get the other things in her life out of her mind and concentrate. She'll probably end up failing the course. I keep telling her, 'Let them know about the situation' but she doesn't want to, as it upsets her so much even to talk about it.

So what can students do – and how can we help them to do it?

We offer some thoughts below. You'll be able to add many more ideas, specific to your own subject and discipline.

Activities before lectures. You can advise students to:

- Look at the course programme to see what topics will be coming up.

- Think about what signposts were offered at the end of the previous lecture (if this is one of a series) and recapitulate what they learnt in the last session.
- Identify what they already know about the topic of the coming lecture.
- Make a short list of questions about the topic, to have in mind during the lecture, with the plan of checking which ones have – and which have not – been answered in the lecture.
- Try to get hold of any references in the course documentation that are cross-referenced to a particular lecture, and glance through them.
- Ensure that all the tools necessary for the job are on hand: paper, pen, highlighter, electronic notebook, ruler (eg for looking at balance sheets in Accounts), any handouts issued in advance (eg in the course booklet), something to rest on (eg a clipboard or hard-covered file).

Activities after lectures. You can advise students to:

- Annotate their notes (but not write them out again!), using a high-lighter pen to mark key areas and underline the main points.
- Make brief headline summaries on cards of key points to act as aids to memory and revision.
- Have a quick look at what other students have written down and discuss with them why they have written things differently, if this is the case.
- Look through their notes for any areas where they were muddled or unclear, and seek clarification (in textbooks, on the Web, via electronic discussion boards, by asking each other, by taking it up with the lecturer, and so on).
- Look for links between this lecture and the next ones coming up in the series, so they can be thinking ahead.
- Look for links between this lecture and other lectures on other modules being studied at the same time, so they can make connections.
- Check out what assessment activities are critical to the learning from this lecture (exam questions, essay topics, practical class tasks, and so on).

We recognize that for many students achieving absolutely all of these things would be unrealistic as they struggle to balance study with other demands on their time. However, in our experience, providing students with this kind of guidance is helpful to those with, perhaps, no tradition of higher education in the family, for whom being at university or college is an alien experience. They may not be able to do every one of these tasks, but being made aware of the kinds of activities that help students to get a good degree (or even just to cope) may be very reassuring. We shouldn't just expect students to understand implicitly what studying in higher education really means. For those who want to take this further, you may wish to recommend to them books specifically designed to develop their study skills, including those by Creme and Lea (1997), Northedge (1990), Northedge *et al* (1997), Race (1995, 1999b, 2000) and Rowntree (1998).

The next chapter looks at how lectures relate to other parts of students' learning and investigates the ways in which we can aim to give students a joined-up learning experience. This can be a difficult task at a time when the curriculum has frequently been atomized by modularization, unitization and semesterization, let alone when the conflicting pressures on teaching and learning support staff simply to keep the higher education show on the road seem to mitigate against a cohesive approach!

9

Linking lectures to other teaching/learning activities

The fact that this book is mainly about lecturing should not blind us to the fact that lectures are only one dimension of students' learning experiences, and indeed only one part of our own teaching experience. In some ways, lecturing is a common factor across a wide range of disciplines (although not all subjects make wide use of lectures as a teaching method). The other ingredients that make up the mix of our students' learning – and our own teaching – are far more diverse across disciplines. It could be regarded as a problem that lecturing gets such a high profile, both for us and for our students. Indeed, students can fall into the trap of regarding the agenda we cover in our lectures as 'sacred', and all the rest of the things they do as less important. Bligh (2002) has suggested that:

> How to link lectures to other methods is an issue much neglected by teachers and not well covered elsewhere in the literature. …lectures teach information. Tutorials, practicals, etc teach other skills based upon that information. The secret lies in designing tasks (eg problems for discussion) that will practise the skills (eg criticism, evaluation, analysis, application of principles, decision making and so on). A major problem of curriculum design (distinguish this from syllabus construction) is how to progressively build skill upon skill and relate it to successive lecture topics.

Some of the issues that lecturers raise about links with other kinds of learning provision are aired below.

the lecturers ...

Dr D

Well, yes, I suppose my lectures are the central part of my course. Students are expected to make this the focus of their work, and then follow up the content of the lectures by getting stuck in to reading the papers and tracking down the references, and then getting on with the assignments.

Professor Oakwood

The lectures are down to me, but once I've done my part, there's not much more I can do. I don't see most of the students outside of the lecture room – or not so that I can talk to them by name. My colleagues get on with the tutorials and seminars. Sometimes colleagues will talk to me to clarify what the students are expected to know about a topic in advance of a set of tutorials, but really I have to leave it to them. I make sure, however, that I do at least some of the seminars myself.

Bill

I'm the first person to agree that the real learning has little to do with the lectures. It's in the labs that students get a feel for the subject. Practical work brings it all to life for them. And I can talk to them in the labs, as I go around the benches, watching how they tackle the experiments. I get to know them there – and they get to know me there far better than when I'm at the front of Theatre 2. But some of the students don't seem to have got anything out of the lectures, so I end up on Thursdays explaining things to them in twos and threes that I tried so hard to explain to the whole class on Monday.

Dr Arbuthnott

Getting my lectures right takes up most of my teaching time. I don't have much contact with students outside the lectures. We don't really have tutorials any more. We used to, but with 240 students it's just not on. We have problems classes, which are optional, for those students who need help with particular topics – we timetable these carefully, to match the lecture programme. However, the students who come to these aren't always the ones who should have come. I can't help it if students don't find out that they've got a problem until it's too late to do anything about it.

Louise

I've problems enough with trying to keep up with my lectures. Tutorials are less of a problem, but the groups vary so much from one to another, and there are never as many students actually turning up as on the list. Three of us run the tutorials, and I guess we all try to respond to what the students want to know. Sometimes they're full of questions, and then the tutorials go well. But what can you do with a group of six students who have nothing to ask? Do they know it all already? They soon show that they don't – the coursework sorts that out.

Arthur

Getting the balance right between lectures and other things? I know where I prefer to be – in the studios, of course. Students can't learn art and design just by watching me show them things in a big stuffy room, or by listening to me talking about it without them being able to ask questions. In the studio, I have everything I need. I can put things round the walls, dig them out of drawers and point to particular effects, and show students exactly what we're thinking about. They can ask, 'How on earth was that made?' and I can show them. My desk in the corner of the studio is my home. I've a shared staff room, but I can't talk to students easily there, with my colleague busy at his desk. In the studio, students know where to find me.

Anya Wilenska

Of course my set of lectures are just part of the module. My colleagues who do other parts do this in their own ways – it would be boring for the students if we all did the same. I know that at least two of them spend a lot of time making handouts – slaving over a hot photocopier I call it! But handouts are spoon-feeding. Students have to sort out the information for themselves and turn it into their own knowledge. I can't do that for them. I make sure that they've got quite enough information on the intranet, then it's up to them. And how can I tell whether I'm saying the same things about a topic as my colleagues? Does it matter? Surely the students have to make their own minds up. Nor do I feel I should probe my colleagues about what they cover in their lectures – I wouldn't expect them to be spying on me.

A very mixed picture! Some lecturers believe strongly that the real learning in their subjects takes place far beyond the lectures. Others just assume that everything else outside their lectures will take care of itself. And what do students think?

students' views ...

The word is around that if you attend all of the lectures, and get really clued up on what's covered in them, you can get a 2.1 if you work hard at it. To get a first you've got to be brighter than me! So I go to all of the lectures, despite how boring some of them are. I actually enjoy the lab work far more, and feel that I am really learning something there, but I get worried that it doesn't count anything like as much as the exams at the end.

You wouldn't know they worked at the same university. One week you get a practical and then two weeks later you get the lecture from another guy that tells you what it was supposed to be all about. Why can't they get their act together? I thought this lot we're supposed to be clever people!

I'm good at exams, and am aiming for a first. I use the lectures as a barometer. I go there to find out what I'm supposed to be learning. I then dig deep in the library, and practise answering old exam questions, to get a grip on what I'm likely to be asked. Yes, I still go to the practicals, but I just try to get by there. I can't be bothered with the repetition – doing similar things three weeks running after I've found out how to do it once. And the prac work only counts for 10 per cent, and is only really taken account of in borderline assessment cases, I've heard. I'm in the business of not being a borderline!

We got these lectures and then when we saw the essay titles, one of them was identical to the title of the lecture we did in week three. So I chose that one and based my essay on what she said, but in my own words of course, and I got a lousy mark. What on earth does that mean?

What bugs me is that the lecturers just don't seem to talk to each other! They cover the same thing in different ways in their lectures, even in the same week. And when it comes to the tutorials, the guy taking them has a quite different approach. Who are we supposed to believe? And the seminars – tell me for goodness sake what a seminar is supposed to be. Most of ours are just more lectures. True, the lecturers set us up with things to prepare, but as soon as we start, they interrupt and take over. We'd learn more by having a go at it ourselves.

So where do lectures fit into the bigger picture of teaching and learning?

When considered in the overall perspective of the design of courses, and the curriculum as defined by the intended learning outcomes our students are to achieve, despite all the situational and process-related problems that we've tried to address in this book so far, the overriding problem could be simply that lectures have been assigned far too much importance or that no-one has really thought through where they fit in the overall curriculum.

It is worth reminding ourselves that the historic act of 'lecturing' started way back in the days when literacy was limited, and the principal way of helping people at large to encounter information (and turn it into additions to their own knowledge) was for those who already had the information to *read it out* to those who could not read it for themselves or did not have access to it on their own. It can be argued that the process of 'reading out the information' proved to be such a powerful one that it became embedded in the fabric of our teaching and learning systems in higher education, and perhaps has far outlived its real value.

However, we can respond that it is still very worthwhile to have whole groups of students in one place at the same time, and to use the occasion to provide appropriate shared experiences for them, particularly those which relate to their ongoing studies in all sorts of other learning situations, and which allow them to bring together, share and discuss how other aspects of their learning are fitting together.

In other words, lectures can be an integrating medium in alerting students to the real meaning of the learning outcomes they are intended to achieve, and to the kinds and levels of the evidence of achievement they will be expected to provide so that their learning can be accredited and documented. That said, only some of the learning associated with the intended learning outcomes can ever be realistically achieved *during* lectures: all the rest needs to relate to the wide range of other contexts in which students learn.

Yet it has become the custom to link the intended learning outcomes mainly to lecture programmes. This has the effect of students regarding lectures as perhaps too central to their perspective on, and evidencing of, these outcomes. Correspondingly, it can have the effect on lecturers that lectures are the prime means of 'covering the syllabus', addressing all of the learning outcomes.

As we have suggested in many parts of this book, when challenged about what they do in lectures, many lecturers shy away from actually getting students involved in lectures, using the reason (excuse?) that 'I've got to cover the syllabus. I just haven't got time to stop every now and then and let students try things out sitting there in the lecture. They've got to get on and do this on their own.'

We would argue that it's not the lecturer concerned who has to get through the syllabus, it's the students who have to, and they can only at best 'get through' some aspects of it in your lectures. Therefore we suggest that you only try to 'cover' some parts of the syllabus in your lectures, but cover them well – in other words design those lectures so that your students master some key aspects of it right there in your lectures. That means that in your lectures you spotlight just *some* of the intended learning outcomes, and help your students to at least make a good start on achieving parts of those there in the lecture room. Get them started with such enthusiasm, if you can, that they leave the lecture room fired up to continue on their own to consolidate that achievement and build on it.

In other words, much of the achievement of the published intended learning outcomes of any programme of study necessarily extends far beyond the lecture theatre. But the lecture is the occasion when (ideally) all the students are together. So it is arguably the best time to articulate the intended learning outcomes, explain them to students, and clarify the standards that are implicit (or indeed explicit) in the outcomes. More important, the lecture environment is arguably the best place to help students to map when, where and how their achievement of the learning outcomes can take place, only a little in the lecture itself, and much more in the students' further study actions, independently and collaboratively, in tutorials and seminars as well as libraries, study-bedrooms, laboratories, studios, field trips, workplace environments and all the other learning environments that they are intended to experience.

While it is natural to use a lecture programme as a means of mapping out the picture of intended learning outcomes for a module, we need to think about two kinds of learning outcome associated with a given lecture: those that students can reasonably be expected to have achieved by the end of that particular lecture, and those that students can only achieve when they have extended the syllabus elements that may have been spotlighted in the lecture to their own independent study, practical work, or group work, and so on.

Therefore if there happen to be 15 published intended learning outcomes associated with the curriculum area that is to be highlighted in five lectures, it is useful to explain to the students *which* aspects of these learning outcomes they can reasonably expect to have achieved by the end of the lecture, and (more important) *how much* of the intended learning will extend to the various different learning experiences which will follow – tutorials, seminars, independent study, and all the rest. So merely splitting up the intended learning outcomes across the five lectures and regarding this as having 'covered' the syllabus in the lecture programme is a vain and impossible hope.

Using lectures as a shared occasion to map out the ensuing learning activities can get over the problem of students (and indeed ourselves) regarding 'the lectures' as 'the course'. They may well be an indispensable part of the course, when well used. They may well be a highly enjoyable and productive part of the course. But they can rarely if ever be the be-all and end-all of any programme of learning. They can't be 'all students need' to achieve what they have to demonstrate in the associated assessments.

Having thus argued that only some elements of the intended learning outcomes will have been achieved at five-to-the-hour as students leave the lecture theatre, it remains well worth articulating what these elements are planned to be shortly after five-past-the-hour as the lecture starts. But to help students to gain a realistic balance about the expectations we have of them, it is important to use the shared experience of the lecture environment to give students a clear frame of reference about all the aspects of the overall intended outcomes that link on to seminars, tutorials, labs and so on. Having done so in lectures, it remains equally important to pick up the threads in each of the ensuing learning situations. In other words, briefings for tutorials, seminars, practical work and everything else need to remind students of how each particular learning event is intended to flesh out specifically the learning outcomes which may have been mentioned broadly in the associated lectures.

Linking lectures to tutorials

Tutorials historically were opportunities for very small group teaching indeed, typically one or two students meeting with a tutor for an hour or more for intensive discussion and perhaps a kind of Socratic dialogue. This kind of tutorial still exists in a limited number of universities, but is under threat even in this context. Nowadays, a tutorial is most often a small-group event led by a tutor, often following up the content of previous lectures, and extending that content to problem-solving activities by students, or in-depth discussion of matters arising from the lecture, or providing opportunities for students to ask questions about aspects they don't yet understand. Here we are using the term to describe learning occasions of perhaps 5 to 10 students with a staff member (lecturer, professor, postgraduate student) on a weekly, fortnightly or more occasional basis.

the lecturers ...

Marisa

I find tutorials a nightmare! It's not so much the business of turning up and doing the tutorials – it's the matter of linking my tutorials to Jim's. We both run tutorials following up each other's lectures, but I never can tell exactly what he's done other than by borrowing notes from a student. The students tell me that when he does tutorials arising from my lectures, he tends to give them new handouts of his own, but my tutorial students don't get these, and they complain that they're not all in the same boat.

Anya

It's the students – they come for tutorials quite unprepared. They haven't taken any notice of what I asked them to do in the lectures. They sometimes come to a tutorial when they weren't even present at the lecture.

Salima

I hate tutorials. I've just not got the time to prepare for these – it's bad enough keeping up with my lectures. Still, students don't seem to care much about tutorials either, and not many turn up.

Bill

Thank goodness for tutorials! At least I feel I'm getting through to students there. When there are just six or seven students, I can really deal with their questions. I usually prepare a problem sheet for each tutorial and give it out in advance. Most students have at least had a go at the problems and bring their attempts to the tutorials, so I can spend time on the things they found hard.

students' views ...

I went to the first few tutorials, but I wasn't getting much out of them. It seems to me that it's the lectures that count. No one asked me to sign in for tutorials – I don't think attendance counts for anything. Besides, more than once I turned up only to find a note on the door saying, 'Tutorial cancelled this week due to illness'. They don't cancel lectures like that – someone else takes the session if the lecturer is off ill.

I go to just about all of the tutorials – I guess they wouldn't be on the timetable if they didn't count for something. But of course it's never the Prof who takes the tutorial, except once in a while. It's usually one of the postgrads. They are fine at explaining things we don't understand, but they don't set the exam, and I never know how important what we're doing in the tutorials really is.

I'd go to the tutorials if I didn't have to work to pay my way through uni, but something has to give. It was hard enough to arrange my shifts so I could get to the main lectures most weeks. And there was the time I really tried to get to a tutorial where I wanted to get some help with 'heat pumps', and changed my shift, only to find that the tutorial had been rescheduled because of a staff meeting.

Tutorials? What tutorials? They used to run tutorials years ago when the total class size was less than 80, but now we're over 200 they say it just can't be timetabled. The Handbook explains about the 'office hours' and 'surgeries' for those of us with problems, but it can be over a week to wait to find someone who can help, and we've usually helped each other by then – or just let the problem be.

It's just another lecture really. Yes, they ask us if we've got any questions, and answer them if we have. But as soon as the questions run out, we get more handouts and more information to deal with. We worry that if we ask too many questions we'll miss out on the extra handouts, so we keep quiet most of the time.

It depends whose group you're in. I'm lucky, I'm in Jim's group and he takes tutorials seriously. I always know that I've learnt something by the end of his tutorials. But my mate is in Dr Wilenska's group, and says he's always more confused at the end of the tutorial than he was at the beginning.

Towards joined-up tutorial learning?

It's quite depressing talking to most students, and most staff, about tutorials. There are unmet expectations on both sides. Lecturers are, on average, disappointed at the lack of preparation from students. Students are, on average, disappointed that staff don't take tutorials as seriously as lectures. The situation is made worse by the fact that where class numbers have increased dramatically, tutorials have become viewed as a luxury rather than a necessity, and have sometimes vanished. So what can be done to help make better links between lectures and tutorials, where they still exist? We suggest that an appropriate mix of the following tactics can build a strategy for revitalizing tutorials.

Spread out the learning outcomes

If we can make it clear to students that only some of the intended learning outcomes can ever be addressed within the confines of the lecture theatre, and that important parts of the learning outcomes are to be achieved in the context of small-group work in tutorials, it can help students to take tutorials more seriously. Moreover, if the detail of the intended outcomes to be achieved in tutorials is mapped clearly to the tutorial schedule, those students who know they need help with particular syllabus elements can make sure that they attend the relevant tutorials. It is also worth considering legitimizing those students who know they have already mastered the particular outcomes *not* to turn up at those tutorials, though reminding them of the benefits they might achieve by using the tutorials to consolidate their own learning, for example by explaining what they have mastered to others who haven't yet done so.

When learning outcomes are stated and explained at the beginning of a lecture, and summed up towards its end, it takes very little extra time to point out to students the particular aspects of these outcomes that will be addressed in tutorials picking up the threads of the lecture.

Take our own tutorials more seriously ourselves

Students often pick up the impression that lectures count much more than tutorials. This is not least due to students' timetables being largely based on lecture programmes, with tutorials being seen as 'fitted in' where and when possible. However, probably the most significant factor affecting students' attitudes towards tutorials is our own attitudes to them. If we cancel them at short notice when something else comes up (however important), or worse, if we don't turn up punctually or fail to turn up at all, the message to students is clear – second-class learning components.

Work more closely with others following up our lectures

Lack of continuity between lectures and tutorials is probably the most significant turn-off for students. If the person running the tutorial seems to be blissfully unaware of what we covered in our lectures, students quickly gain the impression that tutorials don't count. Ideally, to conduct a good tutorial, the people running them need to have been present at the lecture – not just last year or the year before. They need to be able to build on exactly what their students have already experienced. They need to be in a position to follow up the body language they may have noticed at the lecture – for example those occasions where many of the students looked puzzled. They need to have had time to seek out illustrations and examples that will build on what the lecturer has started. And especially where several people are going to conduct tutorials in parallel, they need to talk to each other so that their students are more likely to gain an equivalent follow-up experience. While it is hard to pin down exactly whose responsibility this liaison really is, the person in the best position to try to address the issue is undoubtedly the lecturer.

Link tutorial content more firmly to assessment criteria

While in some institutions, participation at tutorials may already influence assessment to some extent, it tends too often to boil down to 'benefit of the doubt' discussions at exam boards. If, however, students are aware that tutorials will be their practice ground for meeting assessment criteria, they are much more likely to take tutorials seriously. This of course returns us to the learning outcomes issue. Tutorials need to be occasions where students can see that they are addressing learning outcomes in detail, where they will in turn *evidence* their achievement in forthcoming exams.

Gather and use students' views on tutorials more consistently

Too much of the repertoire of methods we use to gain and analyse student feedback is focused on lectures. We need to be equally focused on the whole range of *other* components of students' learning experience, and particularly on tutorials.

Linking lectures to seminars

The terms 'seminar' and 'tutorial' are sometimes used interchangeably, but here we are differentiating between the relatively small group we have described as a tutorial and the larger group of perhaps 20–30 (and sometimes larger) groups of students we are calling a seminar. Bligh (2002) has suggested that there is often a great deal of confusion between tutorials and seminars. He defines the difference as follows:

> A seminar is a discussion initiated by a presentation (normally at the same meeting, but you could sometimes regard the [preceding] lecture as the presentation). Seminars take place in a business context in a way that tutorials don't. A tutorial is a discussion in the presence of (and

commonly led by) a tutor. So some tutorials are also seminars. That's why so many people confuse them. But there are many seminars that are not tutorials, and many tutorials that are not seminars.

We will continue this discussion of seminars from the position that a seminar is essentially focused around one student (or more) preparing and presenting a contribution, which is then the basis for discussion by the group at large, including responses from a tutor.

Typical comments from staff about seminars might be something like the following.

the lecturers …

Professor Oakwood

The seminar programme is a jewel in the crown of my department. It drew favourable comment at the recent institutional review. It's our way of covering all those things we just can't squeeze into the lecture programme, and students take it really seriously. The best students produce some really good seminars. It helps me to pick out the ones who are most suitable to proceed to research with us. I always set a couple of questions in the exam that are on the seminar programme agenda.

Arthur

Thank goodness we've still got the seminars. We had to give up the tutorials when the numbers grew. The seminars give me the chance to really show students things, where they can all see them properly, and can talk about them and argue and debate. Seminars give us a chance to sit the students down together and get them to discuss and debate properly in a way they cannot in the big lectures.

Salima

I hate doing seminars: I get so bored doing the same thing several times in a week with different groups. I get stuck with so many as I'm the most junior (and expendable) member of the department. I lose track of who I've done what with and it always amazes me that what took me an hour to do at the beginning of the week is all done in 40 minutes with the last group.

Dr D

I think it's important that seminars aren't just yet more lectures. I allocate each of my students a research topic, and suggest one particular core paper for each of them to dig out. The problem is that once the student giving the seminar has stopped, no one tends to ask any questions, and the seminar would dry up if it weren't for me taking over and seeing if the presenter really understands it. You also have a problem about what to do if the student doesn't do the preparation or just fails to turn up. Then the onus falls on me again, I'm afraid.

Dr Arbuthnott

With a big group, we can't let all the students give seminars – there's just not time. So I divide them into seminar groups of eight, and get them to work together. It's up to them whether they all join in the presentation, or whether some do the preparation and others the delivery. They're really quite good – some of them link up to the Web live in their seminar presentations, and some have designed computer simulations to illustrate what they're presenting. I allocate each group a mark – all the students in the group get the same mark, as I can't possibly tell whether they contributed equally, that's up to them to sort out.

students' views ...

I wish someone would tell us exactly what a seminar is! I've asked my friends on different courses, and even at different universities, and no one comes up with a clear picture of what a seminar is, except that it's not just a lecture. For one of our lecturers, it's when we give individual presentations to the tutorial group, for others it's when someone gives a talk to a larger group, and for some it's just like any other session where we're supposed to have read up about something and then the lecturer talks about it instead, and never checks up what we've read (so we don't, of course).

The frightening thing about these seminars is that you never know whether the Prof will turn up when it's yours. If that happens, and you do well, it's a good thing, and you've scored brownie points if you're heading for a Master's next. And if you blow it, you've no chance. But you can work your socks off, and if the Prof doesn't turn up, no one really notices how hard you've worked. It's a lottery.

There's a wide range of seminar topics posted, and we 'book' the topic we want to do. Then the timetable is posted. If you're one of the first, it's a real sweat trying to get it ready in time, before the stuff has even been touched on in lectures. But if you're last, it's worse – you're still slaving away getting the seminar ready when everyone else has their head down revising for the exams, and you probably won't get more than two or three in the audience on the day. Another problem is that what seems to be a straightforward topic can turn out to be a real nightmare to get to grips with. Where do you stop with following up references?

It's the group working that bugs me. It's ok in groups of three or four, we can all split up the work. But eight! It ends up that two or three of us do the work, and the rest just sit back and do naff-all. It's not fair that everyone gets the same mark.

I'm scared stiff of giving a seminar. I've never spoken to a group before. I don't mind lectures, I don't have to make a fool of myself there. In tutorials it's ok as it's a small group and I know the other three, so I can join in now and then. But speaking to 20 people for 15 minutes? I wake up shaking at the thought sometimes. I've so far avoided it though. I was part of a group seminar, and I did all the preparation of PowerPoint slides – I enjoyed that. It went well too.

It's the time it can take that's the problem for me. Some of the topics seem to be way off the syllabus, and it's hard to know what to do with the bits and pieces when preparing for the exams – you can't go over it all again, no way. The only bit you really know is the one you prepared yourself. With the best will in the world you can't make notes at all the other seminars too. In any case, they're not all brilliant, and you might take notes and get it all wrong.

Seminars: freeing students up, or tying them down?

There are many good reasons for letting students loose on the literature, and having them prepare a presentation then give it to their colleagues. It's good practice for research. It helps them to tackle a range of skills that can't be developed in lecture programmes, including:

- becoming more confident at speaking to an audience;
- gaining skills in thinking on the hoof, and answering tricky questions;
- digging in deep to a particular bit of subject area, and making sense of it.

With big classes, it seems impossible to give every student the chance to prepare and give a seminar, and becomes difficult to find enough different topics anyway. When there's a wide range of seminar topics on the agenda, they necessarily stray wider and wider around the core curriculum, so it's more difficult to link the seminar programme to exams and so on. And while with tutorials it is reasonable to expect to be able to relate these to the intended learning outcomes of a module, with seminars it can be much harder.

Yet despite the difficulties, the learning payoff for students can be vital. The learning payoff from seminars is likely to be different for each student as far as subject content is concerned, but much more focused in the context of transferable skills such as literature searching, preparation, delivery and handling questions. When contributions to a seminar programme count for assessment, perhaps it's the transferable skills that need to be looked at, rather than the subject-specific ones? Most students continue to remember the first seminar they had to present. That particular bit of subject content can become firmly mastered, simply as a result of having to present it to others.

So what can be done to link what's learnt through seminars to what's learnt from a lecture programme? We suggest that addressing the following dimensions can help to strike a suitable balance.

The lecture course and seminar programme both benefit from careful linking

For example, when a seminar programme has been arranged, rather than going fully into a particular aspect in the lecture, you can suggest to the class, 'The student preparing seminar F should take a look at this issue, and share thoughts on it there.' It can also be worth linking at least some of the intended learning outcomes for the course directly to the seminar programme, and refraining from trying to 'cover' these in the lectures directly.

Assessment needs careful consideration

If seminars don't count in terms of assessment, there are plenty of students who will take this as a message not to bother with them. But if they do count, how do we make the assessment valid and fair? Validity is the least of our problems here: seminar assessment is likely to be based on what students have actually done in their preparation, and what they are seen to do in their delivery and question-handling. Fairness is more of a problem, in that if a series of seminars takes place over several weeks, it is no surprise that the later seminars will reflect all sorts of things that students have learnt from witnessing each others' triumphs and disasters. The standard almost always rises progressively over a series of seminars, as students gain knowledge, experience and expertise from watching each other's efforts. So should the assessment criteria be progressively more demanding? That would be hard to defend at an exam board!

Perhaps the simple solution is for seminar assessment to be essentially pass/fail, where students who make a serious attempt pass, and students who put no effort at all into it (or absent themselves from it) fail. This can take a considerable degree of the strain away from those students who may be most at risk from seminar assessment – those who give it a good try, but aren't yet very good at it. This allows them to use their own seminars as a learning curve. Even with pass/fail assessment, it is still possible for those witnessing the seminars to spot real talent, which can be taken into consideration in other arenas, such as when advising students about choices that may be open to them or suitable for them after the course. Moreover, having a pass/fail assessment system is one way of addressing the fact that the seminar agenda can rarely be a level playing field in content terms. Giving a straightforward seminar really well is then no worse than having an earnest but laboured stab at presenting something that is really tricky. (Perhaps we should remind ourselves of this regarding our own lectures!) However, there are some who would argue that a simple pass/fail approach provides no incentives to do more than a 'good enough' job.

Assessment can be shared with students

Involving students in their own assessment can deepen their learning. Moreover, it can sustain their interest and concentration. For example, with assessed seminars, peer-assessment can be really useful, especially for helping students to develop the processes involved in giving presentations and handling questions. Peer-assessment gives students something to do at other students' seminars, long after they may have given their own seminars. Self-assessment of seminars can also be really useful (especially if it is used as a basis for dialogue with a tutor, rather than as assessment *per se*). Getting individual students to reflect on what they have learnt from the experience of preparing, delivering and defending a seminar presentation can be a deep learning experience, and useful in equipping them for the next time they meet similar learning situations.

Students can need help with the time- and task-management associated with seminars

Perhaps the most significant danger is that students can put far too much energy into preparing a seminar, at the expense of keeping their grip on the curriculum at large. They can end up disadvantaged in exams simply because of this. One way of addressing this issue is to have all seminars in the first half of the duration of a module (provided of course that no other parallel modules are bringing in summative assessment at the same time). But this can bring the disadvantage that seminars are being prepared and delivered before important topics have been addressed in the lecture programme. This can be turned into a virtue, of course, if the lecture programme can be responsive to what has actually occurred in preceding seminars, picking up points of confusion that might have arisen in the seminars (without making the students concerned feel put down).

Minding all those other gaps!

So far in this chapter we've touched on just two common aspects of higher education programmes – tutorials and seminars. We've already seen that while it is within the bounds of imagination to link tutorial content to intended learning outcomes (and overall assessment), it becomes much harder to do so for seminars. But there are many other curriculum elements that play their part in courses, including laboratory work, field work, independent study, distance-learning elements, intensive short courses, computer-based learning elements, online learning elements, case-study work, work placements, project work, group work, and so on. There's a lot more to most programmes of study in higher education than a series of lectures with some associated tutorial or seminar work.

Take laboratory work for instance. In many courses in science, engineering and several other disciplines, students may well spend more time in labs than in lectures, tutorials and seminars put together. They have their closest contacts with teaching staff in lab sessions, particularly with those demonstrating and supervising their work. Such students may also spend more time writing up lab reports than they spend on any other kind of coursework. Much of the content of their lectures may link to practical work. The need to make carefully planned links between theory and practical work is critically important. For example, students may be unable to make sense of some of the experimental work they do in labs until the relevant theoretical background is provided through the lecture course, so careful timing is needed to make sure that students don't end up not understanding what they are trying to do in their practical sessions. Therefore it is really useful for the lecturers who are responsible for the theory sessions to know exactly which aspects will relate to students' subsequent practical work, and to make these links clear in their lectures. Similarly, it can bring a topic to life if during a lecture some practical data obtained from the lab (perhaps by previous students) is used as the basis for analysis and interpretation exercises, so that students find out in advance how to investigate the data they will themselves collect in due course.

Practical work normally takes its place in the assessment profile leading to an award in science or engineering disciplines. However, while it may be necessary to 'pass' the practical components, it is usually the case that formal examinations (and even other coursework components) are most important in terms of credit towards a degree. Yet with students spending so much time on practical work, they can fall into the trap of not leaving sufficient revision time to get to grips with the theoretical aspects of their subjects in preparation for exams. While it is true that outstanding students who look suitable for proceeding to postgraduate study are often first noticed through their practical work, we need to help students keep an appropriate balance between the time and energy they devote to practical work within the overall effort needed to lead safely towards a degree.

Apart from practical work, many of these other 'gaps' between lectures and parallel course activities are minded by their associated assessment. Discrete elements of a course are often separately assessed, and students can gauge how much of their energy should reasonably be devoted to these elements by how much they count for in the overall assessment picture. It helps students enormously to have the intended learning outcomes of each and every course component spelt out clearly and understandably. More importantly, it is vital for students to gain a feel of how much each of these areas is worth in the big picture of their assessment. But we need to make sure that students really take ownership of those parts of the picture that they are expected or required to tackle on their own, without 'teaching', particularly independent study elements of their courses.

There remains the issue of linking each and every of these curriculum elements together in some meaningful way. They may well already be linked to the scene set by intended learning outcomes, each playing its own role in developing students' skills, competences, attitudes and knowledge in well-specified directions and dimensions. But these links are likely to be clearest in *our* minds. We need to help paint the big picture in ways where it becomes clearer to students themselves. When and where is the best time for us to try to do so? In our lectures. That's where we have all of the students in the same place at the same time. That's when we can use tone of voice, body language, emphasis and so on to colour in the picture of how all of these disparate learning experiences should link together for students.

Perhaps the 'mind the gaps' agenda is, in many subject disciplines, that elusive purpose for having lectures in the first place. Perhaps this

157

is what we should be concentrating on in our lectures. The lecture can be where the big picture is addressed. The lecture theatre can then become the briefing zone, relating to all of the course components, not just the arena in which to focus on particular aspects of information in a bid for it to be transformed into student knowledge.

10 Inclusive lecturing: encompassing diverse students

The lecture room is at first sight a place where everyone has an equal opportunity to learn, but this is not necessarily the case. Students in universities and colleges often have a range of disabilities, some of which we are likely to know about and others which, either due to the nature of the disability or because of students' (frequent) reluctance to mark themselves out as different, we don't know about. As well as a human commitment to ensure all our students can benefit from the learning experiences we offer, in the UK at least there is legislation that makes it unlawful for us to discriminate against students on the grounds of disability (Special Educational Needs and Disability Act 2001, www.hmso.gov.uk/acts/). The following sound-bites give an idea of some typical issues lecturers may face.

the lecturers ...

Arthur

Last week the student services woman came up to me just before my lecture and said, 'You've got a profoundly deaf student in your class, so I've told her you will provide all your lecture notes to her in advance. That's all right, isn't it?' Well, no actually it's not all right, because my lectures don't work like that. When I'm showing slides, I make comparisons, draw inferences, ask students to identify influences, that kind of thing and the notes I use are just the bare bones, often just the list of slides. The trouble is, to show the slides to good effect, you've got to have the lights down, which means she can't lip-read. We had a bit of an argy bargy about it, and in the end I suggested that the student makes a tape of each lecture and gets it transcribed. If she then uses the slides in the slide library alongside that, she'll get a much better picture of what's going on, even though it's a lot more work for her.

Dr Arbuthnott

When I'm talking through diagrams on screen, I rely very heavily on the visual image, and I've been told that this makes it difficult for students who don't see well. What I've been asked to do now is provide my PowerPoint slides prior to the lecture for the lad concerned, so he has a chance to scrutinize it on his own screen. It's a bit a of a pain, because it means I need to be a week ahead with my preparation, but it's all good discipline, I suppose.

Professor Oakwood

As far as I am aware, we don't have any disabled students. We did have a chap once who couldn't use the stairs, but he left after the second year. Anyway, all our classrooms now have wheelchair access, so we're covered on that one.

Anya

I have had students come up to me saying that I go too fast and that they can't make notes properly because they are dyslexic. Surely that's not my problem, it's student services' responsibility. I've got no intention of doing all the work for my students. It's their job to learn.

Louise

This one guy, who always creeps in at the back of the room at the last minute, keeps pestering me to give him my lecture notes in advance of the lecture. But I'm often fine-tuning up to the very last minute, so I can't do that. Life's hard enough just trying to keep up with the preparation, without these unreasonable requests.

students' views ...

I have a registered disability, but just because I'm not in a wheelchair, it's as if I don't exist. They seem to think that just because they've provided wheelchair access to the lecture theatres, they've done their stuff. But I find it very difficult to sit in those dreadful seats for 90 minutes at a stretch, which is what we get if the lecturer decides to skip the break and finish early, so he can get back to his research.

There are signs up all over saying, 'No eating or drinking in the lecture theatre' but I'm diabetic and need to eat at 12.30, so I bring my sandwiches. I've had filthy looks from the lecturer more than once, but I don't see why I should have to explain myself.

These whizz bang lecture rooms are fine for most people, but when the lecturer is using the data projector, the main lights are dimmed and she's speaking from the console in semi-darkness, so I can't see her face clearly to lip-read, and I miss a lot of what is said.

When he asks us to get up and put our Post-its on the side wall so he can collect our responses, I hate it. I know I can ask someone to take mine up for me, but I can't go and look myself at what others have done. The places they've made for wheelchairs are very isolating too, so when he wants us to work in groups of three, two people have to come and stand by me so I've got someone to work with. They can't just turn round in their seats like everyone else in the lecture theatre.

I've had to really struggle to get here and I'm seriously thinking about giving up. The lectures are the worst bit because with the course materials, textbooks and material on the Web, I can pace myself and take my time, but in lectures everything is so fast, I just feel really stupid and it's hit my confidence badly.

When he's showing his slides he sometimes says, 'You can read this bit yourselves, rather than me reading it out to you' but I can't. I hate that!

I had a panic attack in a lecture theatre the week my father died. I just couldn't get out because I was in the middle of a row. Since then, I need to be at the back on the end of a row, but this isn't always easy. I tend to skip lectures sometimes if I can't find a place where I feel comfortable.

It looks so rude sometimes when I fall asleep in lectures. Since I've had ME I feel exhausted all the time, but I'm determined to keep trying. I feel very embarrassed though.

The range of disabilities that students in our classes are likely to experience is similar to that in the population at large and the number of hidden disabilities is substantial, even though the proportion affected in higher education, at around 4 per cent, is less than the 10 to 20 per cent in the population at large. Most of us would say that we are happy to try to accommodate the special needs of any of our learners, even though this sometimes means extra preparation and time. However, it is really difficult if learners with disabilities don't make their needs known to us. The best solution is probably to keep in mind the whole range of special needs our students are likely to have in trying to learn in lectures and to frame our activities to accommodate all students, whether they have disclosed disabilities or not. We provide here some suggestions for lecturers to this end. Much more information and advice can be obtained from your own student services or learning support departments and also from national initiatives such as the JISC TechDis Service (www.techdis.ac.uk) and the National Disability Team (www.natdisteam.ac.uk).

Hearing impairments

These can vary from profound deafness to slight hearing loss. Many lecture theatres are nowadays equipped with induction loops that make it possible for students to pick up signals from the audio equipment directly into their hearing aids. For this reason, where microphones are provided it is helpful if you use them, even though you are confident that your voice will carry without amplification. If you hate being tied down to a podium microphone, check whether a radio version is available that you can clip on to your belt with a throat mike attached to your clothing. Rather than asking, 'Can you hear me at the back?' and then ploughing on regardless, it is a good idea to ask students who have difficulty hearing you to let you know as soon as possible, privately either in person or by giving you a note. You can then address the issue to the best of your abilities.

It's also helpful to try to stand in a well-lit area when speaking, so your face can be seen. There's normally no problem when using an overhead projector, as it lights up your face well enough and the room isn't usually significantly darkened. But when using slides or PowerPoint presentations, you're likely to deliberately dim the lights at the front, and it's much harder for students to see you. Sometimes there's a spotlight at the side you can use to keep yourself visible. If you know there are students who need to lip-read, it can be worth carrying in a desk lamp, and plugging this in at the side and going there when you're explaining your slides. In general, however, it's useful to consciously avoid covering your mouth with your hands, papers or anything else. Additionally, information technology systems are being developed that will allow the lecturers' spoken word in a lecture theatre to be transcribed onto personal devices such as laptop computers or personal digital assistants (PDAs).

Sometimes, particularly in public presentations or large open lectures, you may have a sign language interpreter working alongside you. These are highly skilled people who are trained to interpret what you are saying in real time for people in the audience who cannot hear you. It is an exhausting job, requiring high levels of concentration, so they often work in pairs taking turns. It can initially be rather distracting when you are lecturing to have someone else on the podium working alongside you in ways that may be unfamiliar to you, so it is worth talking to the signers in the minutes before you start and asking them how best you can work together. Then talk to them again after the lecture and ask them which things you did were straightforward for them to handle, and which caused them problems. This can help you plan for the next occasion where you know you'll be working alongside interpreters. When working in these circumstances, it is courteous to introduce the interpreter to the class (do not ask the interpreter to introduce himself or herself). If you are in one-to-one discussion with a deaf student, always speak directly to him or her and not to the interpreter, and remember that the interpreter is a few words behind.

Sight impairments

For students with sight impairments, enabling your lectures to be taped may be helpful, but it is not the only or ideal solution for all. With software now so well developed, the provision of your slides or notes electronically in advance or post hoc can be very helpful, as they may have computers that can 'read' your work aloud to them.

Don't assume that all students who have sight impairments can read Braille, although for those who do, providing written documents in a form that can be turned into Braille can be a great help.

For students who have some sight, it can be important to let them choose where they sit in the room, so elaborate schemes to rotate students' seating positions in the lecture room to encourage more interactive group work in lectures may have to be modified.

Colour blindness

Although colour blindness is not normally regarded as a disability, students' abilities to distinguish between colours can be problematic if colour is a key feature of your presentation, particularly for brightly coloured backgrounds with coloured text in PowerPoint presentations and in elaborate diagrams. For dyslexic students too, the use of certain colour combinations can be unhelpful. One of the most common forms, red-green colour blindness, is almost certain to affect at least some students in any large group. This has implications for overheads or slides: avoid using red and green to contrast bad and good points, which is a natural enough thing to think of doing.

Dyslexia and other specific learning difficulties

This is the most commonly notified disability within UK higher education. In 1981 there were about 200 students known to have dyslexia in British universities. By 1991 the number had increased to around 2,000. In 1997 HESA statistics indicated about 12,820, with numbers rising. However, these figures are derived from institutional returns and the real figure may be much higher for a variety of reasons, including non-disclosure. While it is possible, if time-consuming, to cater for students you know to have dyslexia-related problems, perhaps the real problem is that in any large group of students there will be some who are partially aware that their problems are caused by dyslexia or other specific learning difficulty such as dyscalcula or dysgraphia, or they may not be able to name the problem even to themselves.

It can therefore be worth finding out more about the particular challenges dyslexics can experience, and try to take steps to take these into account as a matter of routine in preparing handouts, overheads, slides and so on. In particular, for example, moving on quickly from one word-based slide to the next leaving some students only part way through writing it down can be problematic, although you cannot be expected to wait for the slowest writer. The best bet is to provide some kind of back-up, either paper-based or electronic. We have heard from colleagues who began the practice of e-mailing handouts, PowerPoint slides and lecture notes to students, fearing that students would not turn up at their lectures, but finding in fact that attendance increased. This could be not least due to the way in which they used the actual lectures as large-group tutorials, based on the materials students had already had, and were able to bring to the lectures relevant topical discussions on matters that had just hit the headlines in the press.

Mobility impairments

Whenever we think about students with disabilities, the most common image that comes to mind for many is that of the wheelchair user, and today most universities have made it possible for these students to access most (but not all) teaching rooms. You may, nevertheless, like to check out for yourself the seating positions that are made available for wheelchair users to see what the sight lines are like and to ensure that they can get the most out of your lectures. Lectures are often static experiences for students, but where lecturers try to make sessions interactive, it is worth remembering that easy mobility is not universal. If you want students to work in pairs or triads, keep in mind the needs of those students who may not be able to leave their seats easily. It's not just a matter of making sure that these students have the chance to participate in buzz groups or syndicate tasks. Remember that they can find the additional embarrassment of needing to be treated differently in any way in lectures annoying.

Mobility issues are much wider than those associated with wheelchair use and may include students for whom getting into the lecture (and getting out again) may be a slow and painful process, so the lecturer who teaches right up to (or beyond) the last minute of the hour, allowing little time for changeovers, can be regarded as being very inconsiderate. Late arrivals at your lectures may be because of difficulties getting across to a different building in a short time, with perhaps a necessary comfort stop en route.

The design of the lecture theatre may be unhelpful too, with seats that are badly designed and with either badly placed benches or nothing at all for students to rest their papers on. For students with arthritis, holding the file or clipboard and trying to write on it at the same time for a full hour can be painful and problematic.

Mental health issues

Claustrophobia, agoraphobia, depression or other mental health issues may make your lectures a nightmare for some of your students. It may have taken a huge effort of will to get to your class at all, and being picked on for being late, inattentive or not participating may be the last straw, particularly for students whose confidence is at a low ebb. The ways in which we ask students questions in class need to take account of the difficulties some of them may experience in feeling they are exposing themselves by speaking in public. We would argue that it is usually better to give everyone a little preparation time to answer a question ('Everyone please try to write down the most important contributory factors that explain this phenomenon'), to watch who is writing and then to choose volunteers to respond who make eye contact with you, rather than to pick on respondents as part of a control/disciplinary strategy.

Hidden impairments

As the number of mature students in higher education increases there are likely to be more students with hidden disabilities including diabetes, heart disease, asthma and other conditions that may make life difficult for them. The nature of hidden disabilities is that we usually do not know about them, hence the need for our practice in lecturing to be inclusive as far as reasonably possible to take account of students' needs. In a modern inclusive society it is not enough to assume that no students with disabilities attend your classes. You simply do not know, and it may be that the students do not label themselves as disabled.

A diverse crowd

Inclusive lecturing is about responding to the spectrum of different needs that any crowd of human beings will present to us. Some of these are visible to us, others are not. Some of the needs are well known to their owners, others are not. We need, however, to continue to cater for the diverse range of abilities represented by our students too. We know, and they know, in any large first-year class for example, that some of them will not be there in the second year. For some it is a matter that they don't really want to be there, and will have exercised their own choices of options resulting in what we call their 'failure'. For others, however, they give it their best shot, and do want to continue, but just don't manage to pass. While we may not, with the best will in the world, be able to teach so well that everyone who wants to will pass, there will always be some students in any large group whose success depends far more on us than we may imagine, and we need to include in our approach any tactics we can that will help them.

What about the workers?

As lecturers ourselves, we may share some of the challenges that impact on students with disabilities. Most lecture theatres assume that the lecturer will stand for the whole presentation, which is not easy for many. Those among us who are short often find that consoles in lecture theatres make it impossible for more than the tops of our heads to be seen if standing in a position where we can fully use the IT, and wheelchair users are likely to be completely invisible if indeed they can access the console. The most common industrial injury for teachers and lecturers is damage to the voice/throat/larynx and lecture rooms are where most damage occurs.

The same legislation that relates to the student experience in the UK also applies to lecturers, so there is a responsibility on our employers to help us to do our jobs, whatever our special needs. The scope of this book does not allow us to offer detailed advice to lecturers with disabilities (nor are we qualified to do so) other than to suggest talking to institutional advisers in Human Resources, Equal Opportunities, Staff Development or Personnel departments to find out ways in which the conditions in which we work can be adapted or ameliorated to help us effectively promote student learning in lectures.

In the last chapter of this book we will look at ways of finding out if we are doing so.

11 How do I know how I'm doing?

Just about everyone who teaches in higher education would love to be really good at lecturing, to be the kind of lecturer whose students write glowing evaluations of them and to be greeted by a warm sea of eager faces every time they appear in the lecture theatre. Not many achieve this and indeed students tend to be much more vociferous in their negative comments than their positive ones. What is most frightening is the number of students who expect lectures to be boring.

How can anyone obtain realistic feedback from students and peers on how our lecturing is going? This chapter is concerned with finding out how we are doing and using this information to help us do the job to the best of our abilities. First we'll look at some typical comments from lecturers.

the lecturers …

Bill

I always dread the course team meeting when we get the student reps to come and discuss the evaluations. People don't want to meet your eye and it's really embarrassing when anything negative about yourself comes up. The students are mostly very kind in public, but what I sometimes read on the forms makes me feel like giving up.

Dr Arbuthnott

Never have any problems, mate. My lectures always go down a storm. In fact, the lot running the new lecturers' course get me in every year to show them how it's done, using the new technologies. Students come up to me all the time and say how much they like the video clips. Although funnily enough, this isn't always reflected in the course questionnaires.

Dr D

When I get the evaluation sheets back, it's really depressing because quite a few times there's more than 60 per cent of the students who describe my lectures as adequate or poor, but I never really get any more information about what this really means.

Marisa

I often forget to give the questionnaires out at the end of the course, and they make such a stink in the Quality Enhancement Unit if we don't complete the paperwork for the annual review, so I often end up having to mail it out to the students by hand and surprise, surprise, get very few forms back because they've all gone off for the summer or whatever. The only ones who ever bother to send anything back are the bolshie ones with something nasty to say, so I don't set great store by their remarks.

It's often very hard to get students to take course evaluation seriously. Here are some of the kinds of comments they frequently make.

students' views ...

As far as I'm concerned, it's a waste of time filling in the questionnaires. To my knowledge, Dr Wilenska's been getting crap ratings for as long as she's been here, but it doesn't seem to make a ha'p'orth of difference. What happens to them once we hand them in? They might as well go into a black hole as far as we're concerned, because we often don't see that particular lecturer again so can never tell if what we said had any impact.

We have to fill in the tick sheets at the end of the last lecture when we're all desperate to get to the pub. You start out trying to do it properly and then as it goes on and on, you just shove down the first thing that comes into your head.

It's difficult to make sensible responses to some of the questions and they never ask about what you really want to say, like 'He's a patronizing, sarcastic, miserable git, who knows his stuff but apparently hates being dragged away from his research to talk to us, so just goes through the motions!' It doesn't really matter; no-one reads them anyway, as far as I can tell.

If they give me one more questionnaire to fill in I'll throw up. I feel as if I've been questionnaired to within an inch of my life. Enough is enough!

Even with a really great lecturer you feel you can't just tick down the excellent boxes, that's just too cheesy and makes you look as if you're sucking up. So you look for a couple of areas where you can tick the 'satisfactory' box to even things up a bit.

Feedback or evaluation?

'Course evaluation questionnaires' are used quite widely in higher education institutions. But what do we get by using such instruments? The questionnaires themselves just give us feedback. Evaluation is much more sophisticated, and depends on tracking significant trends discerned through the feedback, and monitoring the success of changes made to address important issues discovered from the feedback. We need to remind ourselves that if the feedback is given in 'surface' mode by students already bored to death by filling in such questionnaires, then the feedback is hardly likely to be worthy of more than superficial scanning, and should certainly not be regarded as data of validity warranting statistical analysis!

There are many more ways of eliciting feedback from our students than merely using questionnaires. And it is our students who know best of all how well (or how badly) our lectures contribute to their experience of higher education – not least their learning. So feedback and evaluation are important, and we need to strive to make them fit for purpose – the main purpose being, in the context of this book, so that we can prepare and give our lectures even better next time round.

Getting and using meaningful feedback on lecturing from students and peers

What kinds of instruments can we use to find out how we are doing? How can we get feedback from students that has the potential to make a difference? How can we be sure that we are getting the feedback that we really need and not just the feedback we want? These are greatly vexed questions that have no simple solutions. Essentially, methods that are effective at identifying the real issues tend to be time-consuming and difficult to administer, and methods that are administratively straightforward often have limitations in the amount and kind of information they give us.

Methods for obtaining student feedback on lecturing

A wide range of methods exist by which you can get feedback on your lecturing, each with pros and cons, which we aim to rehearse. There are also several valid, and different, sources of feedback on our lecturing. The most important, of course, is feedback from students: they know better than anyone else how well (or badly) our particular contributions to their overall learning experience have been. However, what they tell us may have worrying aspects in terms of how students view learning (Entwistle and Tait, 1990; Williams, 1992; Zelby, 1974 – all quoted in Gibbs, 1998a, p29) and we need to consider how best we use the information we thus gain.

Additionally, colleagues present in our lectures can give us feedback from a different perspective. They, at least, know the problems and issues inherent in giving lectures, and have their own experience to draw on in giving us feedback. Moreover, colleagues giving feedback on each other's lectures almost always report that they themselves learn a great deal that they can bring to bear on adjusting their own approaches to lecturing by watching others' ways of doing it.

Questionnaires

The most commonly used method is some kind of questionnaire, whether used on individual modules/units or ones that cover a whole year or programme of learning.

How can they be used?

Questionnaires, whether paper-based or electronic, ask students to reply to a series of questions, most of which frequently can be answered by ticking a box or selecting a rating from Excellent to Poor, or a corresponding number scale (Likert scale). Sometimes, as well as these closed questions there is the chance for students to write responses to open-ended questions.

What are they good for?

They can be reasonably effective at eliciting comments from students in a systematic fashion, but have a variety of shortcomings and disadvantages. The clearest advantage of questionnaires is that feedback from large groups of students can be gathered relatively efficiently, whether the questionnaires are completed manually in a large group setting, or administered online using appropriate software. A further advantage is that every respondent is addressing exactly the same questions or prompts.

Issues/disadvantages

- Staff are not always very good at asking the right questions.
- Staff ask the questions to which they want to know the answers: their priorities might not be shared by students.
- You only get the answers to the questions on the questionnaire, which may not be the feedback that you really need to know from the students.
- Questions can be framed to get only positive responses (eg 'List three things you have really liked about the lecturer's style') or, sometimes unwittingly, to only get negative comments ('List five ways in which the lecturer could improve').
- Badly designed questionnaires are difficult to administer and to interpret.
- It can be very difficult to get a reasonably representative rate of returns. If you issue them and await responses, most students won't return them. If you insist on them being undertaken collectively, for example in the last lecture of a series, students may not take the task seriously, may rush to get the task out of the way, make unconsidered off-the-cuff judgements that may not accurately reflect their real feelings, get excessively influenced by peers around them, or may simply switch off.
- If you insist on them being completed online before marks are issued, the same issues may apply (and in the UK you might be contravening the Data Protection Act).
- The results you get often depend on how and when the questionnaires are administered rather than what questions are asked or how the students feel about the lectures.
- Questionnaires printed on paper, filled in by students in pen and then collected in are time-consuming and dreary to process.
- Sometimes the hardware/software limits the kinds of questions that can be asked. For example, it is often difficult to get free response questions on forms that are read by Optical Mark Readers. Also, where institutions purchase in bulk OMR carbonless paper on which the course evaluations are printed, question length and number are limited.
- Students get bored to death of filling them in.
- Comments focus on enjoyment rather than learning.
- Comments may focus on factors beyond the lecturer's control, eg 'Noise from the Gloucester Road makes audibility difficult'.
- Students can misunderstand the ratings (Likert) scale and tick boxes that indicate exactly the opposite of what they mean.

- Many institutions use the same questionnaire across all modules and courses. Generic questionnaires of this kind rarely lend themselves to getting in-depth subject-specific feedback relating to particular modules and may indeed ask completely inappropriate questions, for example, for studio-based courses.
- Because large-scale statistical analysis is possible with number ratings, the statistics can easily become the be-all and end-all.

Some suggestions on how to make questionnaires work well to help you know how you are doing in your lectures

- Limit the number and length of the questions and don't ask for feedback too often.
- Collect feedback in the middle of a module rather than (or as well as) at the end of it. This means that students can feel that their feedback can still make a difference to them (not just to their successors), and will be more forthcoming about what is going well for them – and what isn't.
- Pilot the feedback instrument with students and staff before using it with a whole cohort of students.
- Consider getting groups of students to design the questionnaire elements they would like to fill in about your lectures. You'll learn a lot from the questions they design, even more if you dare to use the questionnaires.
- Consider offering incentives to encourage students to return questionnaires, eg a tear-off slip with name and contact details of the person returning the questionnaire to go into a draw for a book token (however, students may need to be convinced that their responses are truly anonymous).
- Use electronic means of processing evaluation, either with Optical Mark Readers or online questionnaires, such as those offered by QuestionMark Perception, to reduce the drudgery of analysis and interpretation.
- Try to avoid using the same questionnaire all the time! Making each different questionnaire context-specific and topic-specific helps to prevent students from just adopting a surface approach to answering the questions, or putting down similar responses to those they used on previous occasions.
- Make sure that your motive (or your department's motive) for gaining feedback on lectures is not just to 'cover everyone's back' or 'have a good paper trail for external teaching quality scrutiny', but to gain data to help everyone make their lectures better.

- Talk to someone about the feedback you receive. Gibbs (1998a, p29) argues that it often helps to have an educational consultant with whom to bounce around ideas derived from student feedback to help us to make sense of what we thus learn.

Informal chats

How can they be used?

These can take place at the end of the lecture, at social events, in the coffee bar, in the lecturer's office or in the Student Union/pub. By definition they tend to be ad hoc, often unplanned, and discussions take their own course rather than focusing on specific issues.

What are they good for?

- Students tend to be more forthcoming on these kinds of occasions than they might be in more formal ones, so you are likely to learn more.
- You've got students' facial expressions, tone of voice, body language and so on to help you discern which aspects of the feedback are really important – not just words, or ticks in boxes.
- Students may also take more time over the process so the responses are likely to be more detailed.

Issues/disadvantages

- It is difficult to know whether the responses you get are representative.
- Students who seek you out may have ulterior motives for doing so.
- Students may not wish to look like creeps and toadies to their peers, so may be reluctant to take part.
- Students may be keener to tell you about your colleagues' shortcomings than your own and this might put you at risk of making unprofessional responses.
- Some contexts may be alienating, inaccessible or even threatening to students with diverse religions, backgrounds or cultures.
- It is likely to be difficult (and probably inappropriate) to make a meaningful record of comments on informal occasions for reflection/action later.
- It is (naturally) much harder to build up a statistically significant body of feedback data, so analysis is necessarily skewed towards the phenomenological and qualitative (but considering widely held reservations about quantitative analysis of low-validity data, this may not be a bad thing!)

Structured or semi-structured individual or group interviews

How can they be used?

Meeting students in small groups to ask a range of pre-prepared questions about aspects of your lecturing can be an extremely valuable way of finding out how you are doing. A further refinement of this can be using a methodology like nominal group technique where students themselves are asked to volunteer areas that they feel are particularly worthy of mention, and then to get students to vote on the issues they feel to be the highest priority, then the next highest, and so on.

What are they good for?

- Finding out what students really want to tell us about our lectures, especially when done with groups of students, so that whoever feels most strongly about something does not have to be the person who voices the issue.
- Allowing us to learn from students' body language, tone of voice, facial expressions and degrees of emphasis which aspects of their feedback they regard as most important.

Issues/disadvantages

- Getting busy students to make the time to come and take part in such an exercise can be difficult, as they may not be able to see the immediate benefit to them.
- There is unlikely to be sufficient time to give all the students in a cohort a group interview opportunity, and excluded students may be resentful, or if volunteers are sought, they may be unrepresentative of the cohort.
- Each interview can be different, even when aided by a standardized checklist of questions. New questions worth asking will come to light over a series of interviews. This makes it difficult to compare across and between cohorts.
- Students may feel exposed. They may wish to go easy on critical feedback face-to-face with the person who has already set their exam.
- This is likely to be a time-consuming method of seeking feedback, both in terms of carrying it out and of analysing the outcomes.

Post-its, post cards or notes

How can they be used?

Students can be invited to give you feedback by means of written, often anonymous brief comments that can be passed to the front of the lecture hall or deposited in a comments box placed at the exit of the lecture room, in the departmental office or outside the lecturer's door. These can be free responses, or you may wish to offer some triggers for their feedback. For example, we frequently give each student (or group of students) three Post-its/cards/slips of paper and ask them to use one to tell us something they would like us to *start* doing, one they would like us to *stop* doing and one they would like us to *continue* doing. Similarly, you could ask students to jot down one aspect of the material in the lecture they feel really clear about and one aspect they feel confused about. You can then follow this up at the next lecture or electronically via a course discussion board.

What are they good for?

- It's a good way of getting reasonably immediate feedback so you have time to troubleshoot or remediate problems before things go too far.
- This methodology is relatively cheap to administer.
- With Post-its in a large-group lecture, for example, a great deal of spontaneous feedback can be gathered in a very short time.
- A small piece of paper or card helps students to prioritize what they really want to say because there's not a lot of room to write at length.
- Anonymity can be reasonably assured – in a large group students will not be unduly concerned about their handwriting being traced back to essays or coursework, though some of the more robust comments may still be muted.

Issues/disadvantages

- You can't expect too much detailed information to result from such an exercise: you are likely only to receive headlines and snap-shots.
- The feedback information you receive can turn out to be quite hard to analyse for trends, as it is easy for you to get distracted by some of the more extreme or unusual comments.
- It is relatively time-consuming to create an authentic-looking data-base of feedback comments, though they can be transcribed and circulated back to students, and stored for evaluative purposes.

Show of hands methods

How can they be used?

This is probably the most frequently used means of gaining an element of student interaction/participation in a lecture. You can ask, for example, 'How many of you now feel reasonably clear about this aspect of quadratic equations?' or, 'Put your hand up if you feel you could now clearly differentiate between the characteristics of Art Nouveau and Art Deco.' These kinds of questions can be used to get some kind of feedback on how your material is being got across to students.

What are they good for?

- High participation levels: raising a hand takes less courage (and effort) than asking a question, so more students will enter into the process.
- Getting an instant response to how your material is being received.
- Enabling spontaneous feedback-eliciting questions to be asked, for example in response to noticing some puzzled faces in the lecture room.
- Identifying broadly which groups of students are having problems.
- Working out which topics to make immediate adjustments to in your next lecture, or to revise.
- Allowing students themselves to see how many of their peers are having the same problems with a topic.
- Giving students a sense of ownership of setting the priorities for the agenda of the next part of their learning.

Issues/disadvantages

- You will only ever get a very general feel, rather than any detailed information.
- Students may be too embarrassed to let on to their peers that they are struggling.
- Students wanting to get a good set of notes might put their hands up to encourage you to get on rather than go over the material again.
- If used too often, students might get into copycat mode, raising their hands when those close to them do so.

Individual electronic feedback/response systems in lecture rooms

How can they be used?

Some institutions have installed into lecture theatres individual electronic response systems in lectures so that each student can be asked to respond via an individual keypad to questions from the lecturer, who can immediately show on screen an analysis of responses from the whole cohort.

What are they good for?

- Bringing some variety into feedback-giving processes for students.
- Maintaining anonymity, so that students feel free to give genuine feedback.
- Quickly computing the proportion of students who are having difficulty with a particular idea or concept.
- You can immediately tell how many students are awake (and whose handset is working).

Issues/disadvantages

- These systems are expensive to install and are still relatively rare.
- The kinds of questions that the lecturer can ask tend to be relatively simple such as picking one answer from five, ascribing a number score, answering yes/no, etc.

Methods for gaining feedback from peers

the lecturers ...

Bill

The idea of having someone come in and watch me teach makes me feel nauseous. I can't imagine I could possibly behave normally. It would make me feel even more nervous than usual.

Dr Arbuthnott

I think it's a great idea for some of the new ones to come in and see how an expert does it. Can't see what I could learn by going and watching some fresh-faced postgraduate struggling on with the first years, though: it would be like pulling teeth!

Professor Oakwood

I can't see any harm in letting some of my junior colleagues come in with a clipboard to watch me teach, but I'm afraid I wouldn't have time to spare to go and sit in on their classes. I'm sure they're all doing perfectly well without me interfering.

Anya Wilenska

It's ridiculous! What exactly is the point? Nobody in my department apart from the Dean understands my subject material, so how can they comment on what I am teaching?

Arthur

What price academic freedom now? I don't want to let the quality police come sniffing round my lectures! I had a talk to my union about it. They advised me to be careful about refusing outright to participate but I'm blowed if I am going to make it easy for them. There's ways of passive resistance I can use, you know.

Peer observation schemes

As the comments above might suggest, most people feel some level of anxiety about having a colleague sitting in the classroom watching what happens, especially when this observer is there as part of a quality assurance, review or inspectorial role. However, getting a supportive colleague to come along to your lectures for the purpose of peer review is a different kettle of fish altogether. It is increasingly common today for colleagues to be involved in peer observation of each other's teaching, a methodology that is likely to provide a supportive environment for constructive criticism. This is particularly so in the UK as external quality review is being overtaken within departments by lighter touch approaches where institutions can demonstrate that they are taking quality enhancement seriously.

Your peers can provide you with lots of information about your lecturing and may well be uniquely placed to comment on the way in which you present your material, as they are likely to be familiar with the content, the students you teach and the context in which you work. As lecturers themselves, they are likely to have a good idea about what is and what is not possible and so will be in a good position to offer a well-informed critique of your lectures.

How does it work?

Typically small groups of lecturers agree to watch each other teach for one or more sessions, with time allowed in advance to discuss what approaches will be used both by the person giving the lecture and by the observer, as well as time at the end for discussing and unpacking the session. Sometimes they use a checklist or review sheet, examples of which can be seen in Brown *et al*, 1993. Otherwise colleagues can agree between them on particular aspects of their work to focus on in a specific session. These might include:

- I would like you today to take special note of how I am asking and answering questions from students, to ensure that these are questions that probe student learning and don't just test out simple recall.
- Look especially at my use of audio-visual aids and tell me how these are coming across at the back of the room.
- Focus please on my voice and my audibility: I want to know how my voice is coming across in this big room with bad acoustics.
- Watch what students are doing within my lecture: are they making notes, listening attentively, undertaking the tasks I set, or are they on planets of their own? Which parts of my lecture seem to be engaging them most?
- Please concentrate today on watching whether I am paying equal attention to males and females, students from different ethnic minority groups, the noisy and the quiet ones. (Asking someone simply to note the gender/ethnicity of students you address and seek responses from in a lecture can be a salutary experience, even for those who like to think they are very even-handed!)
- Comment on how I do at timing and pacing my presentation. You have a copy of my overheads that I plan to use: could you note on them the time at which I start each and watch out for any parts where I seem to be rushing to get through the material.

Peer observation schemes work best when those involved have had a chance to explore the issues and set mutually agreed ground rules at the outset, with a level of agreement on what are likely to be the mutual benefits. You may wish to explore further the issue of peer observation of teaching by looking at materials by Richard Blackwell at the Generic Centre of the Learning and Teaching Support Network, at http://www.ltsn.ac.uk/genericcentre/projects/peer-ob/ or by referring to Murray's (1997) useful checklist on teaching behaviours (quoted in Gibbs, 1998a, p28).

Mentoring

For some people it feels most comfortable to get a more experienced colleague to give them the benefit of advice based on experience. Asking such a person to be your mentor and getting him or her to attend some of your lectures with a supportively critical brief can be hugely beneficial. The processes are likely to be similar to those used in peer observation, with the advantage that your mentor is likely to be able to offer you the benefit of wisdom and experience gained over a number of years, but with the disadvantage that many people feel that having the chance to undertake reciprocal observations provides few useful co-learning opportunities. Mentors may also be very busy people, so they may find it difficult to free up the time to undertake more than the very occasional session.

For more information on mentoring see Fullerton (1996, 1998).

Course/unit/module review meetings

Many programmes hold annual or more frequent reviews at which feedback from students is presented and discussed. If a course or programme evaluation form is used, this is likely to be the forum in which it is unpacked, and often feedback on individual programmes or lecturers is also presented. Often student representatives are asked to such meetings to provide what is hoped is a representative view of students' comments they have elicited from their peers in informal and semi-formal contexts. Some universities provide training or leaflets to student reps on how to elicit meaningful feedback, often using a combination of the methods above. The quality of the feedback provided will depend on the students concerned. On occasions it can be very robust, but at other times honesty is sacrificed to tact where student reps fear that voicing negative feedback might impact on their own scores and grades.

Fellow lecturers can also use these occasions as opportunities to settle scores, grind axes and ride hobbyhorses! When well conducted, however, they can provide you with really useful opportunities to get comparative information about how your lectures (and other aspects of your work) are going compared with other lecturers, with insights that might not otherwise be made available to you.

Evaluating your own lecturing

There are also ways in which you can evaluate your own lecturing, although this is most likely to be effective as part of a triangulation process with feedback from students and peers. There are a variety of instruments you can use for this, including those in our own *Assess Your Own Teaching Quality* (Brown and Race, 1995) of which a sample page is included in Table 11.1. These readily adaptable grids are designed for users to evaluate themselves against statements, ticking boxes that apply to their own position in relation to the activities listed. They are designed to enable users to be reflective about their own approaches and to clarify which activities are relevant to their own context and subject material.

We'll conclude this chapter with some of the kinds of student comments that we feel to be indicators that our lectures have been productive learning experiences.

students' views ...

I came out of the lecture feeling inspired to go and read some more about the subject.

I can't wait to follow up some of the references she suggested. The first thing I plan to do is rush off to the library to try to get hold of some of the texts she suggested.

Before the lecture I couldn't see how all the different bits of information fitted together but now it is much clearer.

I now look at things rather differently: her approach has made me review some of my preconceptions.

I now know much more than I did before. I feel as if I've made great strides intellectually.

The time just flew by. I couldn't believe it when he started on his conclusions.

Thirty years on from his lectures, I still remember his passion, infectious enthusiasm and brilliance. An interest he kindled then is still with me all these years later and his was only a minor option on my degree course.

Table 11.1 A grid for assessing your own lecturing

Lecturing to large groups	I do this often	I do this from time to time	I can do this when needed	I can't do this yet	I'd like to be able to to this	I don't intend to do this	I don't need to do this	Action plans or comments
I prepare and publish in advance an outline of the aims and content of each lecture session.								
I clarify the aims or objectives of each session at the beginning, explaining the intended learning outcomes.								
I check how many learners already have some experience of the topics included and use their experience wherever possible during the session.								
I devise tasks and activities to be done during lectures, both by learners individually and in buzz groups.								
I prepare clear briefings for the tasks which learners will do during large-group sessions, for example by preparing overhead projector transparencies of the task.								
I gather from the learners the products of their work on tasks they do during large-group sessions, for example drawing reports from selected buzz groups.								

Table 11.1 continued

Lecturing to large groups	I do this often	I do this from time to time	I can do this when needed	I can't do this yet	I'd like to be able to to this	I don't intend to do this	I don't need to do this	Action plans or comments
I clarify the assessment criteria and assessment standards relating to the subject matter in each lecture and explain to learners what would be looked for in exams.								
I put each lecture into perspective in 'the big picture' showing how the content relates to that covered in previous lectures and to forthcoming topics.								
I gather feedback from learners regularly, for example using short questionnaires or Post-it exercises such as 'stop', 'start', and 'continue'.								
I prepare handout materials that save learners from having to copy down things they see and hear, and which contain activities and exercises.								

Appendix:
More definitions of
'lecturing'

In Chapter 2 we presented a selection of people's views on 'lecturing'. Here are many more. You may find it interesting to pick out several trends that recur.

> Asked what I do, I say: 'I lecture, I am a lecturer.' By that I've decided I mean something fairly literal, going back to the roots of the word. Literally, then, when I say, 'I lecture' I mean: 'I read and teach reading.' By 'reading', here, I mean: 'methods of inquiry, ways of asking questions, approaches to thinking and learning'. Lecturing then means something other than standing up and talking (which describes behaviour, not purpose), it means (to me) teaching students to read the world with critical eyes. (A lecturer in languages)

> A mode of teaching which, at its best, offers the possibility of a face-to-face meeting between students and teacher whereby information, experience and enthusiasm for (subject) learning can be conveyed to learners, and audience involvement and feedback generated. (A staff developer about to retire)

> The presentation of a particular viewpoint on a subject under scrutiny, in order to encourage students to think about that subject in new or alternative ways. (Lecturer in performing arts)

> Describing and illustrating important issues using oral or vocal measures. (Lecturer in information sciences and computing)

> Seeking to provide the spark that ignites students' interest and desire to learn on the topic for themselves. (Lecturer in legal aspects of business and management)

> Helping people to learn your subject. Whether lecturing is a profession is an extremely complex question: my feeling is that many lecturers

don't see themselves as professional lecturers, but rather as professional mathematicians, linguists, etc. Lecturing is about students and helping them enter the joy of the subject you teach; this means that you have to enthuse and intrigue the students, so that they want to carry on studying the subject, and want to know more about it. Research is an important part of the lecturing role, but for me the main emphasis in lecturing is on student learning, rather than on the research grants you might be able to obtain. But I know many of my colleagues wouldn't feel that way! (An educational developer)

Lecturing is a million different ways of engaging any group so they leave your session buzzing. (A specialist in TESOL)

To enthuse students in a given subject and provide the highest level of information and support for their learning. (Lecturer in drama)

Presenting in a comprehensive way a subject to a group of people, aiming at transferring knowledge and accommodating learning needs. (Lecturer in computer science)

A rewarding, nerve-racking process involving mental and physical agility. It's entertainment, interaction, participation, with a sometimes unappreciative audience. (Lecturer in materials engineering)

A lecture is a prepared presentation of predetermined length given to an audience who are expected to listen except when invited to question; and is delivered with the intention of conveying knowledge, understanding or values chosen by the person who is lecturing, or by a group of which that person is a member. (A retired professor)

Lecturing is a fossil of the oral tradition – valued like coal or amber – as the students like the collective experience; lecturers like to show off. (A mathematics lecturer)

The presentation of material in a structured manner to assist, direct and inspire learning. (Lecturer in design)

An activity to convey information and understanding in a subject – to convey the 'flavour' of a topic. (Biological sciences lecturer)

Imparting knowledge – method for doing this. (Lecturer in health psychology)

Delivering an interesting and informative presentation on a defined topic, and engaging with the students' response. (Lecturer in history)

My definition of lecturing might provisionally and tentatively be mooted as: 'teaching a subject to a group of learners' or 'leading and managing the process of learning in a group'. (A further education lecturer)

Lecturing: the live, personal transmission of knowledge about a subject by an expert in that subject. (An administrator)

Off the top of my head: talking at or to an audience, imparting knowledge, information – non-participative. (A member of staff of a professional body)

Delivering a structured talk to an audience with the intention of imparting knowledge? (An early retired professor in the field of purchasing and supply)

Two definitions, one broad, one narrow. Broad: teaching at further and higher education levels. 'He's a university lecturer.' 'He lectures at the university.' Narrow: a particular form of teaching, involving imparting information to large groups of learners with little or no interaction by the teacher with the learners, except for 'questions' at the end of a set piece presentation by the teacher. To be contrasted with other teaching approaches such as tutorials, seminars, workshops, laboratory practice, etc. (A senior psychologist/hospital manager)

Lecturing: presentation, usually by one speaker, of information, ideas, opinions, arguments, usually to a large-ish audience. Presumably you don't need to be reminded of the old chestnut about lecturing being the process by which information is transferred from the notes of the lecturer to the notes of the student without passing through the brains of either. (A senior university administrator)

Provision of a formal authoritative discourse to an audience. (Commissioning editor for a publisher specializing in training)

A verbal discourse delivered to engage the minds of an audience in the exploration of hypotheses, ideas and concepts. (A quality enhancement adviser, from a nursing background)

Giving a one-way instruction/lesson on a specific subject. (A senior secretary in an educational institution)

Alternative theatre. (A professional musician)

Speaking from the lectern. (A practising engineer)

Being talked at about things I don't understand (the student experience). (An educational developer)

Communicating knowledge on a specific subject in a coherent manner. Inspiring others. (A psychology graduate working in a leisure centre)

It always seems to be in the afternoon – soporific. (A builder and design consultant)

I feel that the term 'lecturing' is increasingly unhelpful as we move to more 'active' learning approaches – problem-based learning for one. The biggest pitfall of the term is the expectation that it produces for students, ie that they will be 'lectured at'. I suppose if we do stick with the term, it needs emphasizing that it should encompass a whole spectrum of learning and teaching approaches. (A curriculum developer)

Guiding the learning of a particular group of people on specific topics. (A training conference manager)

A formal, tutor-led session in which the main focus is transfer/delivery of information, knowledge, concepts, etc (rather than using, applying, etc) with interaction often limited by factors such as the nature of accommodation and student numbers. (A chemistry lecturer)

When working with new staff I start with defining lecturing as 50–55 minutes of largely uninterrupted discourse from a teacher with no discussion between students and no student activity other than listening and note-taking. Most agree that is a fair representation of the craft as they know it; we then move on to think about how to enhance the process to make it a more active process. But the above is a definition that makes a good starting point. (A staff developer)

A lengthy, informative, one-way verbal treatise delivered by a subject expert; emphasis is on content rather than style. An educational meeting of a subject expert with students during which a number of different learning activities may take place, not all of which may be predetermined, in the context of specific objectives. (A New Zealand open learning pioneer)

I find it difficult to define lecturing per se. I could define 'good lecturing' as the presentation of new ideas that inspire, stimulate thought and provoke action. And I could define 'bad lecturing' as the dull repetition of ideas easily found in textbooks and that takes place because it is scheduled to do so on the timetables of staff and students. (A professor of business management)

A situation where there is an information exchange between a learning facilitator and others. For understanding and learning to take place beyond the exchange of information, the lecturer requires the skill of rapport building and an understanding of learning, which are not necessarily present in all who engage in lecturing! (A staff developer)

A didactic presentation without overt teacher–student interaction. A method appropriate to, but not restricted to, large groups. (An information services manager)

A complete waste of time (unlike teaching). Otherwise known as hectoring or bullying. Reading out notes to students so that they can write them down again. More time-consuming than photocopying and yet more expensive. (A further education learning and teaching development coordinator)

To my mind, 'lecture' is a portmanteau/umbrella term covering an enormous range of practice from the transmission and (hopefully) reception of information through to the interactive and collaborative exploration of knowledge and its potential application. Too often, it seems, the model is locked firmly into the 'Me talk, you listen' model in which the very process of transmitting material is assumed to imply its reception and comprehension. (A professor of educational development)

The activity of lecturing is akin to electromagnetic radiation. It spreads equally in all directions from the source, usually at the centre of a sphere radius R, thus is subject to the inverse square law. The only defence against lecturing for receivers (targets, students, mugs) is distance (sit at the back) or in severely penetrative rays of wisdom, the use of shielding (brick or concrete) walls. Filters or interference patterns (daydreams) are less reliable but sometimes unavoidable. Lecturing can be placed in a continuous spectrum of failed communication, for good or ill:

- terrorism;
- religious fundamentalism;
- bible thumping;
- bigotry;
- lunacy;
- crying in the wilderness;
- preaching;
- teaching;
- telling;
- selling;
- training;

- brainwashing;
- advertising on TV.

(A retired chemist and safety trainer)

Lecturing *isn't* about conveying facts, data, etc, all of which can be done by other means, and doesn't require x people sitting in y room at 9 on Thursday morning. What it is about: a form of educational theatre. A good lecturer models how you think about this subject, conveying through words, body language (and technical props where necessary), the processes of thinking and connecting that characterize whatever it is she or he is teaching... Information comes in as a demonstration of how you organize or question that information. (UK National Teaching Fellowship winner)

Provoking, arguing and confronting a large group of people in a formal and structured way. (UK National Teaching Fellowship winner)

A social interaction which motivates, stimulates, inspires and enables learning to take place – for both students and lecturer. (An Open University senior manager)

The challenge to resolve the tension between transmitting knowledge to students and getting them to think for themselves. Mother: 'What did you learn at school today?' Child: 'Not a lot – the teacher wouldn't stop talking.' (An anonymous contribution)

Doing everything I can in the time available to encourage my students to think, question and learn. (Flexible learning coordinator)

I think the most telling view we have of 'lecturing' is the way we use it in common everyday speech – such as, 'I don't need a lecture from you on that', 'Stop lecturing me about this', which can actually be part of or develop into arguments. If we use this as our basis for a definition of lecturing then it seems a very negative process. Talking at someone about a topic in a superior way. Imposing one's view of a subject on another person. It also conjures up imagery of arrogance and supercil-iousness; even shouting at, being condescending towards, patronizing... Not a rosy picture of student learning I'm afraid! (Staff developer)

I often think that a definition of what something is not can be helpful too, eg: 'Lecturing is not reading word for word from a lengthy hand-out.' (Staff development support staff)

The sharing of knowledge, the development of skills, the exchange of ideas and facilitation of learning. (Dentistry lecturer)

A process by which a person with knowledge shares this with others in a way that is interesting to the learners, and learnable. (Pharmacology lab instructor)

Passing on knowledge to students to make them aware of key concepts in a subject and how to discover more information on that subject for themselves. (A molecular epidemiologist)

Lecturing to me is about initiating thought processes in others by offering stimulating examples. Specifically stimulating curiosity and enquiry, thus leading to learning. (Lecturer in nursing ethics and law)

Sharing own knowledge, own and other's ideas, attitudes and influences with others, in order to increase knowledge, stimulate interest, give theory on which to build (whether agreeing or disagreeing with it), and influence practice. (Lecturer in nursing: learning disabilities)

Passing on information to students in a way that will make them understand – also providing a good set of lecture notes. (Lecturer studying on a PG Cert course)

Experienced, subject-specific guidance to what practices and topics are of key importance to a field. (Lecturer in electrical engineering)

Imparting a large amount of knowledge to large numbers of students in a short time. (Pharmacy lecturer practitioner)

The systematic communication and transference of knowledge and understanding by person A to person(s) B. (Lecturer)

Imparting information and ideas and facilitating learning. (Lecturer)

The passing on of information you have to those who don't, and motivating them to learn more! (Lecturer in ICS)

Facilitating learning by presenting academic material using different media. (Lecturer in business studies)

Conveying information, ideas and skills to a large group of students. (Lecturer in electrical engineering)

Providing knowledge and skills, teaching the skills of learning, enlightening ways of thinking. (Lecturer in health sciences)

Teaching, transferring and assessing knowledge. (Lecturer in computing)

Sharing knowledge and information. (Dance lecturer)

Sharing knowledge, encouraging free thinking. (Lecturer in colour chemistry)

To share knowledge and to help others to develop and grow. Stimulating interest in the listeners so that they become curious enough to go away and learn more about the subject. (Medicine lecturer)

To give a conceptually coherent introduction to a theme. (Geography lecturer)

Lecturing quickly induces sleep. (A retired schoolmaster)

Teaching a group of students about the subject matter, giving an overview of the field, highlighting important points, involving students in the learning process. (Psychology lecturer)

Ideally it is the offering of information by one to a gathered group of recipients, which engages all participating. Often, however, it is merely an exercise in public reading for the lecturer in periods of listening experienced by the audience. (A teacher of English as a foreign language)

Word pictures to a good listener. (Anon)

Lecturing is an attempt by teachers to reach areas normally unreachable. (Anon)

Lecturing: teach and inspire. To bring across knowledge of and enthusiasm for a subject. To guide the learning process for a subject. (Lecturer in molecular medicine)

Lecturing is helping people to learn. It isn't teaching them, necessarily, though it could be. Essentially it's helping people to learn by doing some of the job for them, but leaving the remainder up to them. (Maths lecturer turned staff developer)

Lecturing to me means that there is a person who facilitates a session that has high content and is to a large group of people. It can be interactive, using AV aids and is usually set up with the facilitator at the front of the room. If there were other factors operating, eg small numbers of people, I would chose a different method of delivery. (A New Zealand polytechnic staff developer)

The word 'lecturing' to me implies someone talking to a group, or an individual, without inviting the audience or other person to contribute in any way. A one-way dialogue. (A journal editor in the field of training)

The process of imparting or transferring a huge body of knowledge from an expert (or a more learned person) to a learner (or novice), the learner in this mode of learning often being very passive. Metaphorically, this form of teaching is akin to filling up an empty vessel. It more or less, rightly or wrongly, obviously assumes that the learner has nothing to contribute in the learning process, merely to be 'talked at' and/or told all that he or she needs to know. However, innovative lecturing, the practice which I subscribe to, involves the use of activities such as timed tasks, buzz sessions and questioning, appropriately interspersed within the lecture session, to actively engage the learner in a participative and meaningful learning process rather than being 'talked at'. This approach to lecturing not only motivates the learners but also reduces boredom and creates interest in the learners through the variety of activities. (A staff developer)

Postscript

Reviews of *Lecturing: A Practical Guide*

'A useful volume for those new to teaching. I haven't read it right through of course, but I shall certainly recommend it to my new staff in the department.'

(Prof A E Oakwood)

'I wish I had read some of the advice given in this book before I started this job. There's lots of useful ideas I could use, if I ever get past trying to keep the content up to date.'

(Dr Selima Theodocus)

'It's a relief to see that I'm not the only person who finds lectures a trial. It's been helpful thinking about the student perspective, and there are lots of things about students with special needs that had never occurred to me.'

(Dr W B Evans)

'Who on earth would have the time to do a quarter of the things they suggest? Students coming to university are all adults and they have to take responsibility for their own learning. It's not my job to make it easy for them. In my country, only the very best students go to university, and they don't get this kind of spoonfeeding.'

(Dr A Wilenska)

'Not much here about using the new technology, is there? How about some practical tips on promoting learning using electronic means?'

(Dr G K Arbuthnott)

References and further reading

Anderson, D, Brown, S and Race, P (1998) *500 Tips for Further and Continuing Education Lecturers*, Kogan Page, London

Andresen, L W (1994) *Lecturing to Large Groups*, SEDA Paper 81, SEDA, Birmingham

Barnes, R (1995) *Successful Study for Degrees*, Routledge, London

Biggs, J B (1987) *Student Approaches to Learning and Studying*, Australian Council for Educational Research, Hawthorn, Victoria

Biggs, J (1999) *Teaching for Quality Learning at University*, Open University Press/SRHE, Buckingham

Bligh, D (2000a) *What's the Use of Lectures?* (5th edn), Jossey-Bass, San Francisco, CA [The 6th edition of this book has been published in 2002 by Intellect, Bristol]

Bligh, D (2000b) *What's the Point in Discussion?*, Intellect, Exeter

Bligh, D (2002) Unpublished correspondence with the authors

Bloom, B S, Engelhart, M D, Furst, E J, Hill W H and Krathwohl, D R (1956) *Taxonomy of Educational Objectives: Cognitive Domain*, McKay, New York

Brookfield, S (1986) *Understanding and Facilitating Adult Learning*, Open University Press, Buckingham

Brookfield, S and Preskill, S (1999) *Discussion as a Way of Teaching: Tools and techniques for university teachers*, Open University Press, Buckingham

Brown, S and Race, P (1995) *Assess Your Own Teaching Quality*, Kogan Page, London

Brown, S and Race, P (1998) *Staff Development in Action*, SEDA Paper 100, SEDA, Birmingham

Brown, S and Smith, B (1996) *Resource-based Learning*, Kogan Page, London

Brown, S, Jones, G and Rawnsley, S (eds) (1993) *Observing Teaching*, SEDA Paper 79, SEDA, Birmingham

Brown, S, Armstrong, S and Thompson, G (eds) (1998) *Motivating Students*, Kogan Page SEDA Series, London

Cannon, R (1992) *Lecturing*, Campbelltown, NSW

Chambers, E and Northedge A (1997) *The Arts Good Study Guide*, Open University Worldwide, Milton Keynes

Chalmers, D and Fuller, R (1996) *Teaching for Learning at University*, Kogan Page, London

Cowan, J (1998) *On Becoming an Innovative University Teacher: Reflection in action,* Open University Press, Buckingham

Cox, B (1994) *Practical Pointers for University Teachers,* Kogan Page, London

Creme, P and Lea, M R (1997) *Writing at University: A guide for students,* Open University Press, Buckingham

Daniel, J S (1996) *Mega-universities and Knowledge Media: Technology strategies for higher education,* Kogan Page, London

Drew, S and Bingham, R (1997) *The Student Skills Guide,* Gower, Aldershot

Dunleavy, P (1986) *Studying for a Degree in the Humanities and Social Sciences,* Macmillan, Basingstoke

Edwards, J, Smith, B and Webb, G (2001) *Lecturing: Case studies, experience and practice,* Kogan Page, London

Entwistle, N (1998) Motivation and approaches to learning: motivation and conceptions of teaching, in (eds) S Brown, S Armstrong and G Thompson, *Motivating Students,* Kogan Page SEDA Series, London

Evans, C (1993) *English People: The experience of teaching and learning English in British universities,* Open University Press, Buckingham

Evans, L and Abbott, I (1998) *Teaching and Learning in Higher Education,* Cassell Education, London

Fairburn, G J and Winch, C (1996) *Reading, Writing and Reasoning: A guide for students* (2nd edn), Open University Press, Buckingham

Fox, D (1984) *Personal Theories of Teaching,* A study pack for Trent Polytechnic, Nottingham

Fry, H, Ketteridge, S and Marshall, S (1999) *A Handbook for Teaching and Learning in Higher Education – Enhancing academic practice,* Kogan Page, London

Fullerton, H (1996) *Facets of Mentoring in Higher Education,* Volume 1, SEDA Publications, Birmingham

Fullerton, H (1998) *Facets of Mentoring in Higher Education,* Volume 2, SEDA Publications, Birmingham

Gibbs, G (1992) *Lecturing to More Students,* PCFC Teaching More Students Project Book 2, Oxford Brookes University, Oxford

Gibbs, G (1998a) *H851 Teaching in Higher Education Institute of Education Technology,* Open University, Milton Keynes

Gibbs, G (1998b) *H851 Teaching in Higher Education: Theory and evidence, Chapter 2 Lecturing,* Open University, Milton Keynes

Gibbs, G and Jenkins, A (1992) *Teaching Large Classes in HE,* Kogan Page, London

Gibbs, G, Habeshaw, S and Habeshaw, T (1992) *53 Interesting Things to do in Your Lectures* (4th edn), TES, Bristol

Habeshaw, S, Gibbs, G and Habeshaw, T (1992) *53 Problems with Large Classes,* TES, Bristol

Habeshaw, T (1995) The Art of Lecturing 1, *New Academic,* 4, 1, pp5–7

Johnson Foundation (1987) *The Wingspread Journal,* **9, 2**

Laurillard, D (1993) *Rethinking University Teaching: A framework for the effective use of educational technology*, Routledge, London

Mathew, B, Bolander, K, Mason, C and Morss, K (2001) *Effective Lecturing: A resource for staff developers*, Scottish Higher Education Funding Council

McKeachie, W J (with chapters by Chism, N, Menges, R, Svinicki, M, and Weinstein, C E) (1994) *Teaching Tips: Strategies, research and theory for college and university teachers*, D C Heath, Lexington, MA

Northedge, A (1990) *The Good Study Guide*, Open University Worldwide, Milton Keynes

Northedge, A, Thomas, J, Lane, A and Peasgood, A (1997) *The Sciences Good Study Guide*, Open University Worldwide, Milton Keynes

Polytechnics and Colleges Funding Council (1992) *Teaching More Students, 2: Lecturing to more students*, Oxonian Rewley Press, Oxford

Prosser, M and Trigwell, K (1999) *Understanding Learning and Teaching: The experience in higher education*, SRHE and Open University Press, Buckingham

Race, P (1991) *500 Tips for Students*, Blackwell, Oxford

Race, P (1995) *Who Learns Wins*, BBC/Penguin, Harmondsworth

Race, P (1999a) (ed.) *2000 Tips for Lecturers*, Kogan Page, London

Race, P (1999b) *How to Get a Good Degree*, Open University Press, Buckingham

Race, P (2000) *How to Win as a Final Year Student*, Open University Press, Buckingham

Race, P (2001a) *The Lecturer's Toolkit: A practical guide to learning, teaching and assessment* (2nd edn), Kogan Page, London

Race, P (2001b) (ed.) *2000 Tips for Trainers and Staff Developers*, Kogan Page, London

Race, P, *DeLiberations: Lecturing*, www.lgu.ac.uk/deliberations

Ramsden, P (1992) *Learning to Teach in Higher Education*, Routledge, London

Rowntree, D (1998) *Learn How to Study* (revised edn), Time Warner Paperbacks, London

Saunders, D (ed) (1994) *The Complete Student Handbook*, Blackwell, Oxford

Smith, B (1997) *Lecturing to Large Groups*, SEDA Special No 1, SEDA, Birmingham

Smith, B and Brown, S (1995) *Research Teaching and Learning in Higher Education*, Kogan Page, London

Stone, L, Lytle, G, McConica, J, Morgan, V, Rothblatt, S and Engel, A (1975) *The University in Society*, Volume 1, Oxford University Press, Oxford

Sutherland, P (ed) (1997) *Adult Learning – A reader*, Kogan Page, London

Wade, W, Hodgkinson, K, Smith, A and Arfield, J (eds) (1994) *Flexible Learning in Higher Education*, Kogan Page, London

Webb, G (1994) *Making the Most of Appraisal: Career and professional development planning for lecturers*, Kogan Page, London

Webb, G (1996) *Understanding Staff Development*, Open University Press/SRHE, Buckingham

Willis, J (2001) Past is Perfect, *The Guardian*, Media section, 29 October, p3

Index